the photographer's guide to Washington, D.C.

Where to Find Perfect Shots and How to Take Them

Lee Foster & Ann F. Purcell

THE COUNTRYMAN PRESS
WOODSTOCK, VERMONT

ISBN 978-0-88150-818-5

Cover photos by Lee Foster
Interior photos by Lee Foster and Ann F. Purcell
Book design and composition by S. E. Livingston
Maps by Paul Woodward, © The Countryman Press

Published by The Countryman Press,
P.O. Box 748, Woodstock, VT 05091
Distributed by W. W. Norton & Company, Inc.,
500 Fifth Avenue, New York, NY 10110

Manufactured in China

10 9 8 7 6 5 4 3 2 1

Frontispiece: The White House
Right: The Lincoln Memorial

*We dedicate this book to each other
and to our children as we celebrate
the Washington, D.C., area*

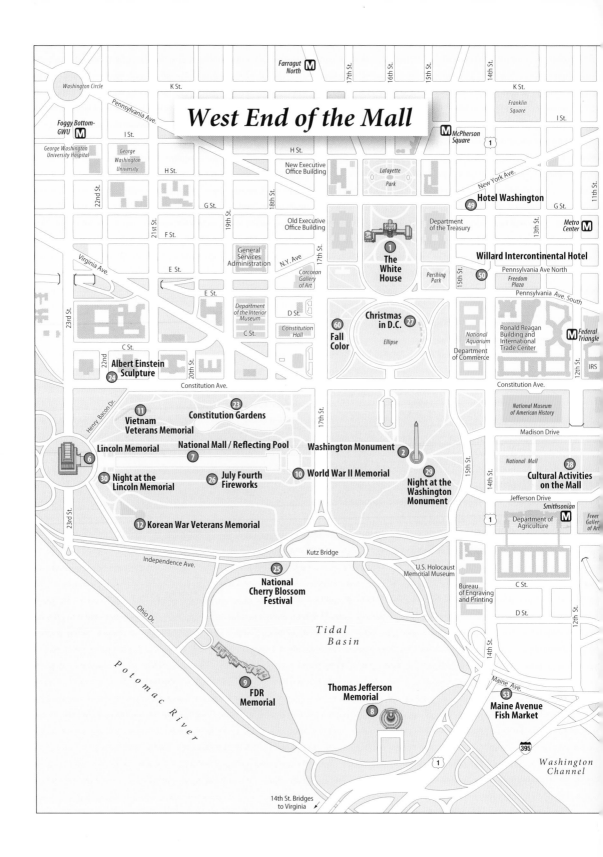

West End of the Mall

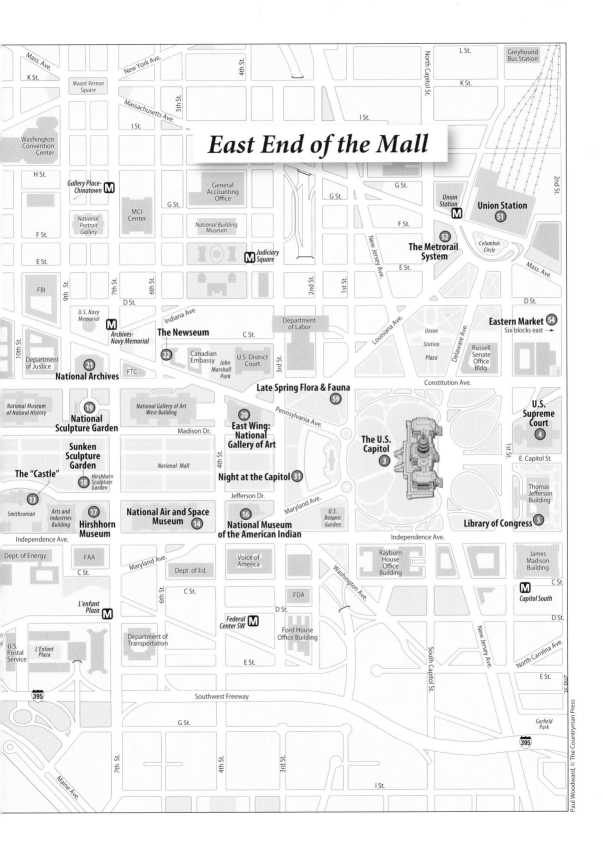

East End of the Mall

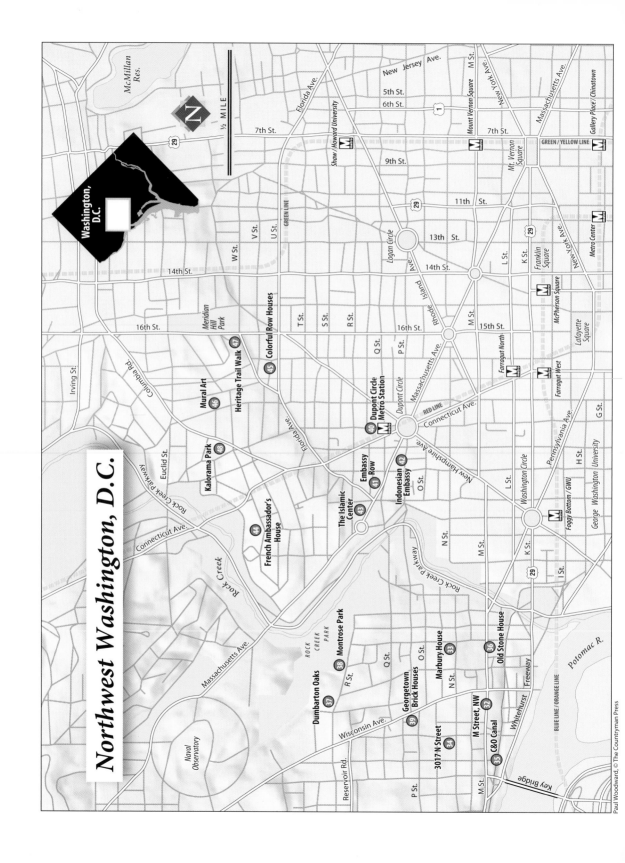

Northwest Washington, D.C.

Washington, D.C.

½ MILE

McMillan Res.

New Jersey Ave.
5th St.
6th St.
Florida Ave.
7th St.
Shaw / Howard University
9th St.
Mount Vernon Square
7th St.
M St.
New York Ave.
Massachusetts Ave.
Gallery Place / Chinatown
GREEN / YELLOW LINE
Mt. Vernon Square
11th St.
Logan Circle
13th St.
L St.
New York Ave.
Metro Center
Franklin Square
K St.
McPherson Square
14th St.
V St.
U St.
GREEN LINE
Rhode Island Ave.
15th St.
Lafayette Square
Farragut North
16th St.
W St.
Meridian Hill Park
T St.
S St.
R St.
Q St.
P St.
16th St.
Massachusetts Ave.
M St.
Farragut West
G St.
14th St.
16th St.
Colorful Row Houses 47
Heritage Trail Walk 46
Dupont Circle
45
RED LINE
Connecticut Ave.
Irving St.
Columbia Rd.
Mural Art 46
Kalorama Park 48
Euclid St.
Florida Ave.
Dupont Circle Metro Station
40
Embassy Row 41
Indonesian Embassy 42
New Hampshire Ave.
O St.
Pennsylvania Ave.
H St.
Foggy Bottom / GWU
George Washington University
Rock Creek Parkway
French Ambassador's House 44
Connecticut Ave.
The Islamic Center 43
Washington Circle
N St.
M St.
L St.
K St.
29
I St.
Rock Creek
Massachusetts Ave.
Rock Creek Parkway
Naval Observatory
ROCK CREEK PARK
Montrose Park 38
Dumbarton Oaks 37
R St.
Q St.
O St.
Marbury House 33
Old Stone House 36
Potomac R.
Wisconsin Ave.
Georgetown Brick Houses
N St.
M St.
39
M Street, NW 37
Whitehurst Freeway
BLUE LINE / ORANGE LINE
Reservoir Rd.
P St.
3017 N Street 34
C&O Canal 35
M St.
Key Bridge

Paul Woodward, © The Countryman Press

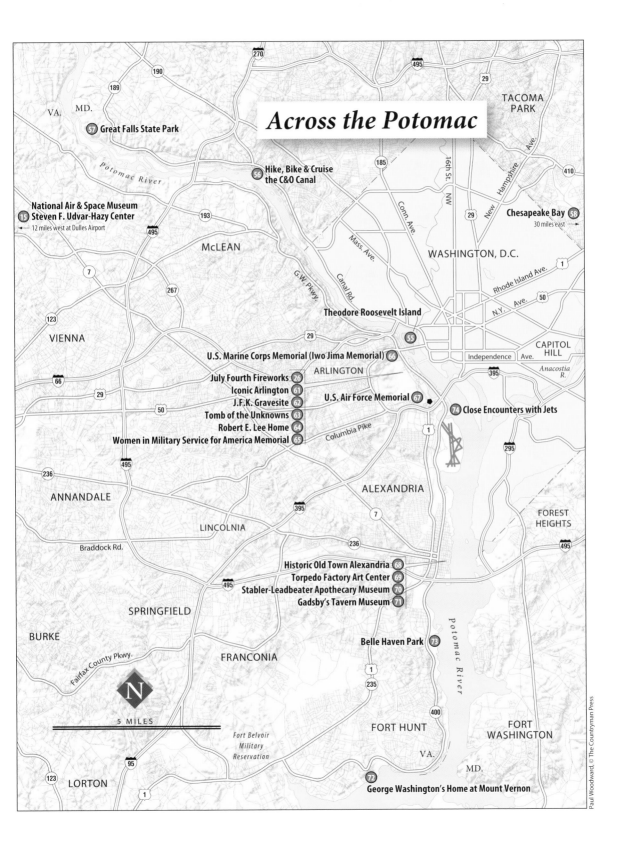

Across the Potomac

VA. MD.

57 Great Falls State Park

Potomac River

56 Hike, Bike & Cruise the C&O Canal

TACOMA PARK

National Air & Space Museum
15 Steven F. Udvar-Hazy Center
← 12 miles west at Dulles Airport

McLEAN

WASHINGTON, D.C.

58 Chesapeake Bay
30 miles east →

G.W. Pkwy.

Canal Rd.

VIENNA

Theodore Roosevelt Island

55

CAPITOL HILL

Independence Ave.

Anacostia R.

U.S. Marine Corps Memorial (Iwo Jima Memorial) 66

ARLINGTON

July Fourth Fireworks 26
Iconic Arlington 61
J.F.K. Gravesite 62
Tomb of the Unknowns 63
Robert E. Lee Home 64
Women in Military Service for America Memorial 65

U.S. Air Force Memorial 67

74 Close Encounters with Jets

Columbia Pike

ANNANDALE

ALEXANDRIA

FOREST HEIGHTS

LINCOLNIA

Braddock Rd.

SPRINGFIELD

Historic Old Town Alexandria 68
Torpedo Factory Art Center 69
Stabler-Leadbeater Apothecary Museum 70
Gadsby's Tavern Museum 71

BURKE

FRANCONIA

Belle Haven Park 73

Potomac River

N

5 MILES

Fort Belvoir Military Reservation

FORT HUNT

FORT WASHINGTON

VA.

MD.

LORTON

72

George Washington's Home at Mount Vernon

Paul Woodward, © The Countryman Press

Reflecting Pool at dawn

Contents

IX. "Natural" Washington, D.C.

X. Seasonal Washington, D.C.: Beyond the Cherry Blossom Festival

XI. Across the River from Washington, D.C.

Introduction

Photographing Washington, D.C., is an opportunity to capture political grandeur, past and present, in the capital city of one of the world's major political forces. Whether you are a visitor wanting to get some good shots of the city's icons or a dedicated professional building a photo portfolio of Washington, this book offers you practical comments about where to go, when to go, and how to get perfect shots.

Pierre L'Enfant's 1791 grand design for Washington called for wide boulevards and plenty of green, open space, showing "magnificence enough to grace a great nation." The height limit placed on buildings, keeping them below the elevation of the U.S. Capitol, lends a human scale. The solidity of the marble and granite structures, many executed with a 19th-century sense of large salon-type space, lends a regal air to the setting. All of this is exciting to photograph.

Washington is also an intense city to photograph because it is one of the great imperial cities of our time, comparable to Beijing or London. What happens in Washington will affect the world. Plus the city is a major repository of American culture, especially with the Smithsonian Institution's 19 different assets.

As a photographer, part of your challenge will be getting a fresh image of such well-known places as the Washington Monument. Remember, no one will ever see it in exactly the light in which you see this iconic place. (You may have to walk around the monument meditatively, viewing it both up close and from afar, but chances are you will make a satisfying portrait of this as well as other historic landmarks.) Or consider that the precise light that you experience over the Reflecting Pool on the National Mall has never been seen; you may

The Thomas Jefferson Memorial during cherry blossom season

stumble on beautiful light and come away with astonishing images.

While Washington, D.C., is perennial, there are always new nuances, making it repeatedly interesting to photograph and experience. Someone who tells you that "the Mall is the Mall; there isn't anything new there" is mistaken on closer view. Consider just two recently opened sites that we discuss: One, the National Museum of the American Indian, has a sinuous outline that presents a refreshing architectural photo unlike anything else in Washington. And the other, the Newseum, has a sixth-story-terrace shooting platform that offers a fabulous, fresh image of the Capitol.

Come. Washington, D.C., beckons. Let us be your guides for a celebratory photo encounter with this remarkable city.

Icons of Washington at night

Using This Book

In this book we've approached Washington, D.C., in a methodical way. Starting with the major icons that any citizen with a camera will want to encounter, we've outlined 11 major themes that might interest you as a photographer—ones that we've enjoyed photographing ourselves.

We realize that readers of this book may fall into one of several groups. Possibly you are a talented amateur photographer, with a capable six megapixel or more digital camera, wanting to get some terrific images of Washington, D.C. With the help of this book, chances are good that you will be successful. Or perhaps, like us, you are a dedicated pro, deeply into the business of publishing photos. In this book we'll give you our best collective judgment on where to go and how to get the great shots in our city. Maybe you aren't a photographer but are accompanying one who's immersed in the scene. Or perhaps you're simply a visual adventurer who wants to see the great views, capture them in your memories, and store them on your "hard disk"—your own mind—forever. Follow this book, and you'll be able to view all the grand sights, from the best angle, and at the right time—even if your camera is invisible.

But be courteous while doing so. Courtesy, when photographing here, has two aspects: your fellow citizens and political/media celebrities. As to the former, the Lincoln Memorial will probably be your most congested moment when shooting in Washington. Allow a little time for people to move in and out of the frame; then be prepared to shoot quickly—to commandeer the area is rude. As for the latter, photographing political/media celebrities in their private moments is definitely taboo here in Washington. We remember one day going

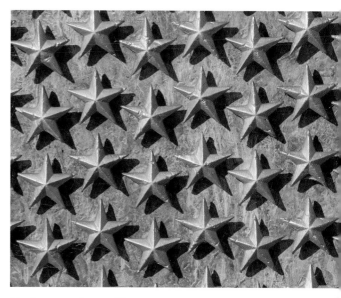

Each star at the World War II Memorial represents 100 soldiers who died

for lunch at a Georgetown restaurant and being seated near famed columnist George Will, who was enjoying lunching with a colleague. It is *not* OK to shoot a celeb in this situation. Washington isn't Nashville. There country music fans literally run up to the stage at the Grand Old Opry and snap photos of the musicians, who would in fact be disturbed if they were *ignored*. In Washington, however, George Will and others of his ilk deserve a little privacy. A quick shot of the restaurant interior would be OK, but be aware of effects of your photo behavior on others in these situations. Learn to photograph quickly and discreetly rather than make a spectacle of yourself.

So . . . whichever category you fall in as a visitor, let's go out and visually capture one of the most intriguing worldwide destinations: Washington, D.C.

The heart of Washington, D.C.

How We Photograph Washington, D.C.

D.C. Is a Walking City

When planning D.C. photography, be aware that this is a walking city, with substantial distances between shots. If your gear is heavy, you'll need to have the stamina to carry it. Learn how to use the Metro, which can get you around quickly. Also, familiarize yourself with tour buses, such as the Tourmobile (their Web site and a few other useful ones are listed at the back of this book). Another provider to consider is Hop-On-Hop-Off, an open-air double-decker sightseeing bus.

Then sit down with a map and plan your time strategically. It's difficult to park a car in D.C., so driving from site to site will occupy a lot of time. If you want to shoot several sites quickly, we've found it's best to get a driver or a taxi with a cell phone who can drop you off, hover or circle, come to pick you up when you call, and take you to your next site.

For example, if you start at the White House, you may look over and see the Washington Monument as an apparent short distance away. But it's actually farther than it looks. A driver can save you the half-hour walk, allowing you to get to other subjects more quickly.

D.C. Is Security Conscious

An unusual aspect of Washington, affecting your gear and photo opportunities, is that the city is highly security conscious. Since the president and the Congress are here, and we are living in the post-9/11 era, this is to be expected. However a second aspect to security is liability. Thousands of people are milling around, and someone might trip over your tripod, making liability a major concern.

Tripods are prohibited in specific areas, especially near the White House, on the Capitol grounds, and at any high-foot-traffic site amid the memorials. The Smithsonian buildings, including the Air and Space Museum, also prohibit tripod use. Test your luck, if you wish, but we have found that security guards at the White House and at the Capitol, for example, will tell you emphatically, "No tripods!" Trying to argue for your "rights" as a photographer will generally not work.

However, tripods *are* permitted by the National Park Service along the National Mall as long as you don't create a liability issue. The shorthand explanation by the National Park Service—which controls much of the Mall—regarding their policy is: "Tripods are allowed on the grass" and on the concrete where there are no crowds. Where thousands of people may be milling about—such as at the Lincoln Memorial, Jefferson Memorial, FDR Memorial, World War II Memorial, or the walkways of the Vietnam Veterans Memorial—you won't be allowed to use a tripod. This makes sense. Yes, we are photographers, but we need to respect public safety. Use discretion with your tripod if you bring one. The park service has no interest in restricting you; they are simply concerned with safety. If a security official says, "No tripod allowed," don't argue. Instead, consider retreating to a less-trafficked area to try for your shot.

Doing night shots of the Capitol and the Lincoln Memorial is possible with a tripod if you step out of the restricted area. Shots of reflecting pools with the iconic structures in the picture are permitted and are exciting to compose. The pool in front of the Capitol is beyond the Capitol grounds, so shooting across the pool at the Capitol is OK.

Wright Brothers' Flyer at the National Air and Space Museum

Sometimes you'll need to ramp up your electronic camera to a high ISO and hand-hold it, as in the Air and Space Museum to photograph the Wright *Flyer*, the historic aircraft that the Wright Brothers flew at Kitty Hawk. A beanbag or a small pocket tripod put on the ground can be useful. Make your own beanbag with two pounds of coffee beans in a Ziploc bag, or buy a small commercial beanbag at a camera store. A beanbag can steady your camera on the ground, on a wall, or on a car roof.

Using a cable shutter release will further reduce shake.

Our cameras and our technology when shooting Washington, D.C., allow for the security consciousness of the site and for the long distances of walking needed, even if we have a driver dropping us here and there, picking us up later. If we have an elaborate backpack for our gear, we know that every time we enter a Smithsonian building, for example, we will undergo detailed searches. Think airport security norms: Leave at home that Swiss Army knife with the corkscrew device for opening your wine bottle. It won't be allowed.

A decades-long tug of war exists between photographers and officialdom over the issue of "permits." If an official asks, "Are you a professional photographer?" it's best to slip back into amateur status to avoid the permit issue. Some controls—not applying to you—are obviously needed to restrain folks like a wedding photographer who tries to set up his several-hundred-person party on the steps of the Lincoln Memorial and take over the setting. This kind of behavior excites the "permit" mentality—as it should.

Our Gear, Your Gear

Advances in camera technology happily put the burden of successful photography more on the eye of the photographer than on the fancy gizmos of the trade. Chances are you have all the equipment you need, and your focus on creativity should move from your equipment to your concepts about what and how to photograph.

When it comes to gear, we are photographic clones of each other. We each carry two Nikon D200 10-megapixel cameras, one with a wide-angle 12–24mm lens and the other with a longer 18–200mm lens. Because of the 1.5x image factor of the digital sensors, this gives us effectively an 18–36mm and a 27–300mm angle range. We believe in redundancy, saving each other in critical situations when we have dropped a camera (it can happen!). Incidentally, because we so often shoot together and have similar images, we won't emphasize attribution of photos in this guide. Both of our collections contain most of the images shown here.

We carry our cameras one on each shoulder, usually under a long shell jacket so that the cameras won't get jostled in crowds, and the lenses won't inadvertently get dirty or wet, as Washington is prone to rain showers. We never change or remove lenses because of the important dust-on-the-sensor issues.

We confine any other gear we might need—as well as water and a snack—to our jacket pockets. Using a camera bag can result in bag-checking issues and longer security-check waits whenever we go into, say, the Smithsonian. Also, we hand-hold most of our day shots, saving a tripod for dusk, night, and dawn shots.

Setting Your Camera for Washington, D.C.

We set our cameras at an ISO of 100 and shoot mainly on Program automatic. Most of our shooting is outdoors in available light. But we do set our ISO Auto feature on the cameras to bump up the ISO as needed in low light, which will occur in dark interior situations, say, at the Air and Space Museum. This allows us to shoot at $\frac{1}{30}$th of a second with whatever sensor sensitivity is required. Aside from available-light photography generally being aesthetically more pleasing, flash may not be permitted in some interior spaces such as museums, where art objects or aging artifacts can be damaged by the light.

In dark interior situations, we hand-hold at $\frac{1}{30}$th and have the ISO ramped up as needed. As stated previously, tripods aren't allowed, although you can sometimes position a beanbag on a ledge or against a column as a substitute.

We tend to shoot everything redundantly with both cameras because each gives a slightly different look, due to the angle/length of the lenses. We also shoot with both cameras just in case there's catastrophic failure of the memory card in one of the cameras, though the likelihood of this happening is rare. A second camera also saves us if we drop one or have a mechanical failure, which also has occurred, though infrequently. And, of course, we always

The Reflecting Pool on the National Mall makes a great backdrop

carry extra batteries, especially in cold weather, when camera batteries tend to drain more quickly.

File Format

Shoot photos at the highest level capture possible, which will be RAW or "fine" JPEG (and possibly both). We shoot simultaneously in the RAW mode and on the highest possible JPEG level. This gives us an immediately usable image as well as a "raw" image that can be interpreted later with utmost variability. This takes larger or extra cards to do our captures, but that is acceptable.

Orient Yourself to Washington, D.C.

It is important to orient yourself to the city as you plan your excursions. The National Mall has an east-west layout, and the White House is on the north side, facing south. This means you will get fairly good sun on the White House for much of the day. The Capitol, at the east end of the Mall, will be backlit in the morning and glowing with light in the afternoon. The Lincoln Memorial, on the west end of the Mall, will be lit in the morning and backlit in the afternoon. Accordingly, you may wish to shoot the Lincoln Memorial in the morning and the Capitol in the afternoon. The Washington Monument, by contrast, can be an interesting subject at any time because of its open site and because it faces in all directions, with sun always falling on it.

There is actually some logic behind the city's street names and numbers. Numbered streets tend to run north-south, lettered streets are east-west, state-named avenues are on diagonals, and areas are designated by quadrants—for instance Northwest is NW. These quadrants are determined by the Capitol building, so, for example, 1st NW means the street is one block northwest of the Capitol.

Light Seasonality in Washington, D.C.

The seasonality of light in on a subject will affect your photo opportunities. For example, a lovely early-spring photo can be made late in the day of the Reflecting Pool, looking toward the Lincoln Memorial from the World War II

Memorial. The reflections can be beguiling, especially at sunset. By late spring the sun will set farther north in the sky. In winter, by contrast, the reflections will be subdued because instead of setting behind the Lincoln Memorial, the sun will set farther south. And, of course, the summer sun will be high overhead whereas the winter sun will be lower in the sky. Another quirky aspect of this shot is that in winter there may be no reflection at all because the reflecting pool may be frozen!

Seasonality can be a special photo delight in Washington, D.C. The Cherry Blossom Festival during the first days of April is, of course, a most congenial time to visit the city and take some exceptional photographs. While walking amid the cherry blossoms along the Tidal Basin, be sure to look in all directions, especially back, when you'll find yourself savoring a delicate view of the Washington Monument framed by branches of blossoms.

You might return to Washington during the fall color and delight in the blazing leaves of the red oaks near the White House, again framing the Washington Monument. A subject as well known as the Washington Monument suddenly comes alive in an entirely new presentation because of the fall season.

Photograph to Enhance Your Life

We see our Washington photo excursions as adventures that advance and enhance our personal education and enjoyment of life. We encourage you to do the same. We are always gathering new photos for our magazine and book editorial work, but we also linger at these sites to better comprehend and enjoy them.

For example, the haunting, aristocratic feel of the Jefferson Memorial rotunda may cause you to pause and recall the greatness of this founder of our nation as you gaze up at his larger-than-life sculpture. You may find yourself drifting back to the day in 1962 when President John F. Kennedy hosted a dinner of Nobel laureates and remarked, "I think this is the most extraordinary collection of talent, of human knowledge, that has ever been gathered at the White House—with the possible exception of when Thomas Jefferson dined alone."

Statue of Thomas Jefferson in his eponymous memorial

Wide-angle shot of the White House

I. Perennial Washington, D.C.: The Major Icons

The White House (1)

Arguably, 1600 Pennsylvania Avenue is the most famous address in the world. George Washington and French architect Pierre L'Enfant selected the site together in 1791. The house became "white" not for aesthetic reasons but to patch up the president's house: White paint was used to cover burned portions after the British torched the place in the War of 1812. Remember that security around the White House is considerable, so allow plenty of time to navigate the barrier system. Be aware that guards are unlikely to allow you to use a tripod.

The main shot to get is through the fence grate on E Street, immediately south of the White House. The lawns and the White House make a pleasing wide-angle shot from this view. Zooming in on the White House can create a dramatic image, day or night. An interesting seasonal shot is of the National Christmas Tree and the White House together. For more information about this iconic shot, see Chapter V.

The Washington Monument (2)

The more you photograph the Washington Monument, the more subtle and variable this icon will emerge to you. The purity of the simple white object against the sky allows for striking graphic photos.

Start right at the base, off 15th Street, and look up at George Washington's grand marble obelisk, 555 feet high, said to be the tallest free-standing masonry structure on Earth. The monument, with its flags and blue sky around it, is held together only by gravitational pull. Mornings 9 to 11 are ideal for a photo as the sun climbs above the treeline. Shoot with a wide-angle lens, including the grass and the sky in your composition. Then walk up to the monument and consider framing it with the flags that circle it.

Later in your travels around town, whether from the Lincoln Memorial or the Capitol, you may want to pull the monument in with a long lens to capture this lone icon. In our discussion of night photography (Chapter VI), we recommend setting up your tripod at the Lincoln Memorial and shooting the Washington Monument as a vertical, with the lit monument shimmering in the Reflecting Pool.

Perhaps you will be fortunate to see lovely late-afternoon or sunset light on the Washington Monument, possibly with some clouds reflecting the same light in the background.

The U.S. Capitol (3)

The regal dome of the U.S. Capitol is a signature Washington, D.C., image that will allure you with endless photographic possibilities. The Capitol is, arguably, the most complicated and satisfying subject in the city to photograph.

Keep in mind that there are three basic approaches: from the west side; from the interior during a tour; and from the east side. From the west side, the classic view is an afternoon-light image, shot from the sidewalk beyond the lawns in front of the building or from beyond the pool between the National Mall and the Capitol.

Two seasonal aspects of photographing the Capitol wide from the west should be considered if the timing of your visit permits. In spring beds of tulips are planted on the west side, and these tulips and the dome can make an interesting photo. Use your widest wide-angle lens, and stop your camera down to a high aperture, such as f/16, to give yourself maximum depth of field. Crouch near to the flowers, and you should be able to get both the flowers and the dome sharp and in focus. In December a Christmas tree on the wide west-side lawn makes a nice shot—though, of course, the National Christmas Tree at the White House is more spectacular.

A classic night shot to consider (see also Chapter VI) from the west side is the Capitol Dome alone or with its reflection in the pool that lies west of the Capitol. During the day, wind tends to disturb the water, but the pool reflection works at night if the winds have stilled.

Next, get an interior perspective during a tour of the Capitol. Free same-day tickets are available at 9 each morning at the Capitol. A tour of the Congressional building is open to all and has its minor moments of revelation. Among the paintings by John Trumbull under the Great Rotunda of the Capitol dome is the painting depicting General George Washington resigning his military command, turning his then-absolute power back to the elected civilian authorities. No general has since had an opportunity to give the Republic a gift of similar magnitude. Consider what would have happened if George Washington had decided at that point—as some had urged him—to become king or dictator. What a different course the country might have taken.

Note and photograph with a long lens the distinct American touch given to the pillars at the original entrance of the Capitol, now the hallway outside the old Supreme Court Chambers. The building's architects decided that the motif should be cornstalks with an ears-of-corn top, not just a copy of some Greek or Roman design—parallel urges to reinvent government *and* pillar design. The old Supreme Court Chambers is one of those Washington places resonant with history. It was here in 1803 that John Marshall affirmed the principle of Judicial Review, then a new concept. And it was here, in 1857, that the Court issued its Dred Scott decision, declaring that a "negro" was a piece of property, which so inflamed the

The Washington Monument from a different angle

North that the Civil War seemed all but inevitable.

Finally, the east-side view of the Capitol is often overlooked by photographers, but it has its own special aesthetic. Major construction and enhanced security on the east side nowadays makes one think that the east-side view is not accessible, though it is actually the front of the building. But we photographers must always think of light and iconic opportunities. For the cover of this book, we chose a photo of dawn light falling on the Capitol dome—the most important single building in Washington, D.C. Here is how you can replicate that cover photo.

A half hour before dawn, get yourself in position on the east side. Parking is easy at this time because the controlled parking period doesn't start until 7 A.M. Park near the intersection of 2nd Street and East Capitol Street. Be sure to bring your tripod and a long lens. Walk down East Capitol Street to 1st Street and set up your equipment. Here's where you'll need to be crafty. The rule for the area—though don't bother to ask a policeman—is that you can use a tripod here as long as you're on the sidewalk. Actually, though, you'll need to be exactly in the crosswalk at 1st Street and East Capitol to get the shot, due to construction issues. So manage your shoot well. As soon as the traffic light turns green, walk out into the crosswalk, quickly set up your tripod—assuming there's no predawn traffic, which there is from time to time—take your shot, and scoot back to the curb. If you don't make a fuss, there won't be any problems. Above all, don't ask a cop for permission to photograph from the crosswalk, which would likely prompt a negative response. As the Capitol glows in the dawn, give yourself an hour to watch the pageant of light unfolding on this most iconic of Washington, D.C., images. Hopefully you'll take home your own cover-worthy photo.

Springtime at the Capitol

The Supreme Court entrance

The Supreme Court Building (4) and Library of Congress (5)

Across the street on the east side of the Capitol are two other major governmental and cultural structures: the Supreme Court Building and the Library of Congress. Both will have the sun on their facades in the afternoon. Effective use of scale here can make interesting photos. For example, try to get an attorney walking alone amid the massive pillars of the Supreme Court Building. The image will illustrate the gravity of the institution.

If you shoot these buildings from the Capitol grounds, remember that guards will probably not allow you to use a tripod, day or night.

The Lincoln Memorial (6)

The setting of the Lincoln Memorial is ennobling: Lincoln is sitting, larger than life, both figuratively and metaphorically. The overall monument is a stately Doric Greek temple, with 36 columns representing the 36 states in Lincoln's Union. The columns seem to embrace the president himself in the interior. Surrounding him are inscriptions of his powerful orations, such as the Gettysburg Address.

It's likely you'll want to get close to the white-marbled Abraham Lincoln sculpture, and then make both a wide-angle shot of his seated presence and a long-lens view of the great man's face alone.

You'll find a lot of people around you, and most of them will want to get a photo of themselves with the statue. So you'll need to be patient and courteous and wait for a few moments for people to leave if you wish to get an uncluttered wide-angle photo.

Night is a more reflective time to photograph Lincoln and is discussed in detail in Chapter VI. But be warned: Even at night, a surprising number of people visit the Lincoln Memorial.

The Reflecting Pool (7)

No site in Washington offers more possibilities for 24 hours a day of photography than the Reflecting Pool, which lies between the Lincoln Memorial and the Washington Monument.

The Library of Congress, with its signature fountain

The Washington Monument as seen in the Reflecting Pool at dawn

Thomas Jefferson Memorial

The soft and diffuse light of early morning, the mirror aura throughout the day if the winds are calm, and late-afternoon or sunset light all present the Reflecting Pool in different and pleasing perspectives.

One good shooting location is from the steps at the Lincoln Memorial, looking toward the Washington Monument. Shoot from the top of the steps with a long lens. Then walk down to the water's edge, around the security barriers, and try a horizontal with your wide-angle. Another good location making use of the Reflecting Pool is from a walkway in back of the World War II Memorial, looking toward the Lincoln Memorial. This can be particularly pleasing at sunset or sunrise, especially if you have some clouds in the sky and the view reflected in a calm pool.

The various meditative photo possibilities are considerable. At night, the Washington Monument with its reflection in the pool is one of our favorite concepts (see Chapter VI).

The Jefferson Memorial (8)
The Jefferson Memorial, modeled on Rome's Pantheon, is stately and austere, honoring this giant of the Virginia aristocracy during the formation of our country.

Visiting the Jefferson Memorial during the Cherry Blossom Festival will be photographically rewarding. The memorial is surrounded by cherry blossoms as you walk around the

Sculpture of Franklin Delano Roosevelt and his beloved Scottie, Fala, at the FDR Memorial

Tidal Basin. Views of the rotunda of the Jefferson Memorial can be framed by branches of blossoms, both with a wide-angle and a long lens. The long lens will compress the blossoms against the facade of the memorial.

At any time of the year, from across the Tidal Basin as you walk along the path, you'll arrive at a certain point where the statue of Thomas Jefferson shows clearly through the columns. This is an engaging photo. Once inside, the 19-foot-high bronze sculpture of Jefferson also makes a good close-up shot, both full body and his head by itself. The sculpture is surrounded by columns.

The interior of this rotunda is shady, so you may need to increase your ISO to make a suit-

able image. Since traffic at this memorial is relatively light, the park service personnel may not be so fussy about a tripod as they assess their wish to assist you vs. their responsibility to protect the public from tripping over tripods. The darkness of this sculpture in normal light also can be ameliorated with the "fill light" feature in the CS3 version of Photoshop, allowing you to bring up the darks without overexposing the lights.

At twilight, this can be a meditative place to photograph, especially if you are fortunate to have a glint of the sun on the roof and if the pool adjacent to the memorial is mirror calm.

Don't overlook the photo possibilities of the Tidal Basin itself. During the day, from April until October, the basin will be full of colorful paddleboats.

Franklin Delano Roosevelt Memorial (9)

The final special memorial to consider during a Washington, D.C., visit is a site dedicated to our 32nd president, Franklin Delano Roosevelt, honoring especially his leadership during the Great Depression. The memorial is located along the Tidal Basin, west of the Jefferson Memorial.

The main photo to get is the sculpture of FDR and Fala, his beloved dog, the largest statue at the site. Other photo concepts would be close-ups of sculptures like *Breadline* by George Segal, which depicts a line of men waiting for a soup kitchen to open. Photos taken in summer, when the sun is high overhead, will be more satisfactory than in winter. Many of the significant sculptures here, especially that of FDR and Fala, are north facing, with tall stone walls behind them, so the winter sun, low in the sky, will keep them in shade.

The memorial has an open-air design that flows through four distinctively designed galleries—outdoor "rooms." Each section interprets a phase of FDR's presidency through murals, waterfalls, and statues of FDR and his wife, Eleanor Roosevelt. Etched onto the red-granite walls are many of the uplifting and incisive thoughts of this articulate man. Look for and photograph his most famous quote, taken from his first inaugural address: "The only thing we have to fear is fear itself."

Sculpture of a soup line at the FDR Memorial depicts suffering during the Depression

The fountain at the National World War II Memorial

II. The Memorials of War

The defining realities of war in the culture of America are a main element to absorb and photograph both in Washington, D.C., and across the river in Arlington, Virginia (see Chapter XI).

The National World War II Memorial (10)
The gravity and vastness of World War II—certainly one of the defining events of the 20th century—will affect you as you review this relatively new memorial. Use a wide-angle lens that takes in the fountain and the stone markers for the individual states. Stand at the top of the walkway on the south end and look north across the monument so that the sun will be overhead or at your back, illuminating the north side of the monument.

Sometimes a close-up photo epitomizes the tragic story of war. Consider a photo of a single star or a cluster of stars at the west side of the monument. Each star represents 100 soldiers who died. At the base of the stars is the poignant message: HERE WE MARK THE PRICE OF FREEDOM.

This evocative and dignified memorial honors the 16 million Americans who fought, the 400,000 who died, and the millions who supported the war at home. A simple statement at the memorial tells the story: "Americans came to liberate, not to conquer, to restore freedom and to end tyranny."

The Vietnam Veterans Memorial (11)
The individual names of the 58,256 soldiers who died in Vietnam are a touching aspect of this memorial, located on the north side of the Mall adjacent to the Lincoln Memorial. Made of black granite, the memorial is a kind of negative space, seemingly carved out of the ground

rather than set on top of it. The memorial is almost a wound in the earth rather than a magnificent artifact—appropriate for a stalemated conflict that never had its victory day. The Vietnam Veterans Memorial attempts to separate the human tragedy of those who served and died from the political issue of U.S. policy in the war.

People tend to come up to the memorial to find a name and share a moment of private grief. This can be a powerful human-interest photo if you can take the photo in a dignified, discreet way with a medium-length lens. Telephoto close-ups of people doing rubbings of the names is another concept to consider. Take the photo with a long lens, focusing on the rubbing, so as to be unobtrusive and not infringe on someone's private grief.

The extent of the loss of life in the war can best be conveyed with a wide-angle shot of this long, low-slung memorial that seems to emerge from the earth. The Washington Monument will appear in the background as you look east.

The Korean War Veterans Memorial (12)

The Korean War Veterans Memorial sits parallel to the Vietnam Memorial but on the south side of the National Mall, slightly in from the Lincoln Memorial. Nineteen stainless-steel soldiers are portrayed walking carefully across rough terrain in a combat patrol. They appear

Tracing the name of a fallen soldier at the Vietnam Veterans Memorial

A wary platoon of soldiers at the Korean War Veterans Memorial

wary and gaunt, suffering from the harshness of the cold as well as the strain of war. However, they are also gigantic figures.

Select an angle with the sun on the soldiers in front of you. To determine an optimal photo for the light during your visit, walk first around all four sides of this memorial. After seeing how the light is falling on the group—so you won't have a backlit subject—consider here two photo studies: Get a wide-angle group photo. Then select a single soldier and do a vertical portrait. Consider also a photo of a sol-

dier with the ghostly wall of unnamed faces in the background.

Unlike the Vietnam Veterans War Memorial, which sought to list every name of those killed in action, the Korean War Veterans Memorial attempts to portray thousands with each face, both the sculptures and the pictures etched into an adjacent granite wall. The United States had 1.5 million Korean War vets, with an estimated 54,229 fatalities. The motto for the monument, etched on the granite wall, is: FREEDOM IS NOT FREE.

Smithsonian headquarters, known as "the Castle"

III. The Best of the Smithsonian

The Smithsonian Institution, sometimes affectionately portrayed as "the nation's attic," is itself reason enough to visit and photograph Washington. English chemist James Smithson bequeathed his fortune in 1846 to the United States to found "an Establishment for the increase and diffusion of knowledge." Little could he have imagined the scope of today's Smithsonian, the world's largest museum complex, with 19 separate entities, including the National Zoo (all discussed in detail at www.si .edu). Several major institutions compose but part of the Smithsonian and are worlds unto themselves.

Keep in mind that reasonable rules of safety will restrict your photo efforts. The Smithsonian doesn't want hordes of people tripping over your tripod, so don't bring one. It's a small price to pay for viewing such a wealth of treasures—and, indeed, the *only* price you'll pay: Admission to all Smithsonian museums is free of charge.

The Castle (13)

The Smithsonian Institution is headquartered in the photogenic "Castle" at 1000 Jefferson Drive SW. Completed in 1855 by architect James Renwick, the Castle is the Smithsonian's first building. The distinctive structure is made of red sandstone from Seneca Creek, Maryland, and is described as Norman in style, a 12th-century combination of late Romanesque and early Gothic motifs. The Castle is a central information point for all Smithsonian photo exploration you may have in mind, though there are tours and photographic opportunities of the building itself and the gardens immediately around it. The information desk and an intro video at the Castle can help you determine your further photographic forays at the Smithsonian's many entities. The **Castle Café,** with its specialty soups and sandwiches, can be a pleasant rest stop between shoots.

The Smithsonian Information Center in the Castle is open daily from 8:30 A.M. to 5:30 P.M.

National Air and Space Museum (14)

The Smithsonian's National Air and Space Museum is one of the most visited museums in the world, with more than 9 million people arriving annually. As is the case with other Smithsonian interiors, the merits of a digital camera will become apparent here at the Air and Space Museum. You will want to ramp up the ISO light sensitivity of the sensor because the ambient light inside the museum is low.

Flight was a new phenomenon for the human animal, realized only in the 20th century. Several icons in the history of flight await the photographer here. View them from below on the ground floor and above from the second floor balcony to determine which perspective pleases you most.

The main entrance lobby contains three landmarks of flight worthy of your photographic attention. First is the Moon Rock. You can touch it and photograph people touching it. This is as close as you might come in Washington, D.C., to an extraterrestrial experience. Second is Charles Lindbergh's *Spirit of St. Louis,* the famous plane that made the first non-stop flight across the Atlantic Ocean. Hanging from the ceiling in the lobby, it photographs well from below because the light on the ceiling is relatively even. And third is the remarkable Apollo 11 Lunar Landing Module, *Eagle,* which was used for the 1969 lunar-landing mission that put the first humans on the moon.

Charles Lindbergh's Spirit of St. Louis *at the Smithsonian National Air and Space Museum*

You can photograph the *Eagle* and *Spirit of St. Louis* together from the lobby level. Then go upstairs to level two and view these legendary artifacts from overhead. From the west side of level two, you can photograph all three icons together, looking down at them from above.

Also on level two is the gallery honoring Orville and Wilbur Wright and their well-documented exploits in December 1903 at Kitty Hawk, North Carolina. On display is their original and famous *Flyer* airplane. The Wright brothers left their home in Dayton, Ohio, with all their self-reliant gear and their aircraft paraphernalia, and set out for the historic launch site. The area was quite remote along the North Carolina coast, and it involved boat access. Their own photographic documentation of the achievement is a masterpiece of our nation's historic photo record.

You won't find it easy to photograph in this gallery, which is a major attraction. Think ISO 1600 at $\frac{1}{30}$th of a second for available light. Possibly bring a beanbag and set it up strategically on the back of a bench with your wide-angle camera and a shutter release. No tripods are allowed.

Exhibit space has long been a fundamental limitation of the Air and Space Museum. An ever-increasing amount of physical space has been required to display the growing collection of air- and spacecraft, and no place on the National Mall could accommodate them. The issue was resolved with the opening of a huge air and space facility, the Udvar-Hazy Center, west of D.C. near Dulles Airport (see site 15).

National Air and Space Museum: Steven F. Udvar-Hazy Center (15)

If you were pleased with the "old" National Air and Space Museum on the National Mall, you will be thrilled with the "new" companion facility, the Steven F. Udvar-Hazy Center, located in a facility at Chantilly, Virginia, near Dulles Airport.

The challenge is getting there. You'll need a car (rental or private), a long taxi ride, or the patience to take public transit. (The Udvar-Hazy Center is located at 14390 Air and Space Museum Parkway in Chantilly. The public trans-

portation option is the #5A bus to Dulles Airport, then a local Virginia bus to Udvar-Hazy.)

The spacious facility—which opened in 2003—consists of a handsome, hangar-type building with 7 acres of floor space and a ceiling height of 103 feet, allowing for creative positioning of their vast flying collection. About 200 aircraft and 135 spacecraft from Air and Space's treasured collection (about 80 percent of its overall holdings) are allocated to this new venue. The new facility has as its mandate presenting the history of aviation and space flight. A visitor's initial impression is that the center has both the artifacts and the state-of-the-art display technique to accomplish that mandate.

Arguably the most special craft to be seen and photographed here is the Lockheed SR-71 *Blackbird*, a spy plane that was the fastest

The Enola Gay *on display at the National Air and Space Museum's Steven F. Udvar-Hazy Center*

and highest-flying jet aircraft ever built. From a second-floor level, you can look down and make a stunning photograph of the *Blackbird*. (You will want to ramp up your digital camera's ISO to get a satisfactory image since tripods are not allowed.) Another famous—or infamous—airplane on display is the B-29 Superfortress *Enola Gay,* the plane that dropped an atomic bomb on Hiroshima in 1945. The oldest aircraft on display is Samuel Langley's 1903 *Aerodrome*. The newest aircraft is the next-generation Lockheed-Martin F-35 Joint Strike Fighter.

Space exploration enjoys its own adjunct hangar at the new facility. The most prominent exhibit to photograph is the space shuttle *Enterprise,* which was the first of the shuttles

Tepee and earthen oven at National Museum of the American Indian

and saw service as a test vehicle but never actually made it into space. Seeing the shuttle up close can't help but remind a visitor of the other clone shuttles, with all their triumphs and tragedies. The *Challenger* and *Columbia* disasters lost both crews and spacecraft.

Bottom line: If you want to photograph significant aircraft in an aesthetically appealing environment, go to the Udvar-Hazy Center.

National Museum of the American Indian (16)

The most photogenic new addition to the Smithsonian presence on the National Mall is the National Museum of the American Indian. Because the mandate of the museum is to portray all the original peoples of the Americas, a visitor will become acquainted here with the Mayans of Mexico as readily as the Sioux of South Dakota. Much thought went into choosing the architecture: A sinuous form of earthen color and texture, faced with Kasota limestone from Minnesota, it undulates and never ends. It's an entirely new architectural look for Washington, D.C.—flowing curves rather than rectangular boxes define the space, making it a breath of fresh air on the architectural scene.

Morning light is best for a photo of this building because the sun illuminates the eastern and southern sides of the structure. View the building by walking around it. A wide-angle lens will be helpful.

Details within the museum also make for interesting photos. A reed canoe in the lobby is appealing. Photograph the canoe close up with a wide-angle lens and from the second floor looking down with a long lens, focusing tightly on the canoe.

When you're ready to take a break from photographing the exhibits, the museum's **Mitsitam Café** features an interesting range of Indian foods from five regions in the Western Hemisphere.

The sinuous exterior of the National Museum of the American Indian

IV. Art, Architecture, and Artifacts

Art and architecture play a large role in the visual sense of Washington, D.C. Some of the most interesting photo possibilities on or near the National Mall are the outdoor sculptures and the buildings themselves. The most striking of these outdoor artworks is an angular red piece by Mark di Suvero titled *Are Years What? (For Marianne Moore)* in front of the **Hirshhorn Museum (17)**. From your position on the sidewalk, this sculpture, north of you, will be a strong image throughout the day because the sun falls on it directly or from the south. If you have beautiful blue sky and a bright sun, you will capture an appealing image. The wider your wide-angle lens, the greater will be your opportunities. Nearby is the **Sunken Sculpture Garden (18),** which boasts another moving sculpture to photograph, Rodin's *The Burghers of Calais.*

Across the Mall from the Hirshhorn are more sculpture gardens, including the **National**

Mark di Suvero sculpture near the Hirshhorn Museum

I. M. Pei's distinctive East Wing of the National Gallery of Art in winter

TV transmission antenna from the World Trade Center at the Newseum

Sculpture Garden (19), next to the west building of the National Gallery of Art. Wander amid these sculptures to discover numerous photographic close-ups. The photographer wishing to discover private, enlightening moments away from the hustle and bustle of Washington, D.C., will find much to celebrate here.

On the north side of the Mall, I. M. Pei's striking, angular **East Wing** of the **National Gallery of Art (20),** which houses modern art, is an artwork in itself, worthy of an architectural photo. Pei's triangle design is a fresh counterpoint to the salon-style grandeur that has been the traditional architecture for Washington institutions. If you happen to be in Washington photographing in the winter, a strikingly graphic photo of the East Wing can be made. Winter will have stripped the leaves of the trees that obscure the building in summer, creating an entirely different aesthetic and an opportunity for a stark, angular, horizontal photo celebrating the purity of this innovative architecture. Your photo will be especially compelling if you have blue sky in the background.

Treasured national historic artifacts are another subject to consider photographing. When standing before, say, the actual Declaration of Independence, the Constitution, and the Bill of Rights at the **National Archives (21)** (700 Pennsylvania Avenue NW), much of what a citizen learns in school becomes suddenly tactile. With a photo, you can take it all with you. One of the original copies of the British Magna Carta has recently been added to the display.

The Newseum (22)

The newest major entity near the Mall is the Newseum (6th Street and Pennsylvania Avenue on the north side of the Mall; www .newseum.org), dedicated to the art of news-gathering and to a better understanding of the role of the media in our lives. Because of the angle of the building, afternoon light falls advantageously on the Newseum's facade and lights the exhibits inside.

A memorable image-of-images to photograph is the **Journalists Memorial** that honors, with their displayed portrait photos, 1,800 journalists who have died in their newsgathering pursuits. Another exhibit shows an armor-plated truck used by *Time* photographers in Iraq until it was ripped apart by a mortar round and riddled with bullets. Astonishingly, the photographers survived. You could spend a half day exploring here. Artifacts to see and photograph include a segment of the Berlin Wall and the 9/11 exhibit, featuring a recovered TV transmission tower from the North Tower of the World Trade Center. The 9/11 exhibit also contains the poignant images of news photographer Bill Biggart, who raced toward the second tower, photographing it until the collapsing tower killed him. Astonishingly, his camera was found, and his photos survived.

Two modern studios at the Newseum are used for current TV news shows, taking advantage of the photogenic location with the Capitol in the background. You, too, can go to the sixth-floor terrace and use this elevated outdoor photographic platform to make an image of the Capitol never seen before the Newseum opened in 2008. On clear days the most pleasing photos of the Capitol can be made shortly before the 5 P.M. closing time.

Constitution Gardens (23)

This green and living legacy honoring the founding of our republic is one of the more tranquil and meditative places to visit on the

Constitution Gardens, a tranquil and meditative place on the Mall

Mall—a far cry from some of the more "block-buster" attractions. Located north of the Reflecting Pool and west of the World War II Memorial, Constitution Gardens consists of an island of rustic greenery in the middle of an artificial lake. The concept of 50-acre Constitution Gardens is to celebrate, with a living tribute, the men who appended their signatures and committed their lives to the breakaway document that sought freedom from the British. Fifty-six men signed the Declaration of Independence. In a semicircle of stones, each of their signatures is writ large. The site was dedicated during the 1976 Bicentennial as America sought to reaffirm the vision of freedom sought by the heroic founders of our country. The photo to get would be a horizontal of the semicircle of names plus the lake, with the Washington Monument in the background.

Albert Einstein Sculpture (24)

The Mall also has its quirky artifacts. Near the Lincoln Memorial, across the street on the north side of the Mall, is a much-beloved sculpture of Nobel Prize–winning physicist and mathematician Albert Einstein, in which the great man is portrayed in an almost huggable, tweedy manner.

Sculpture of Albert Einstein—one of the more whimsical works of art on the Mall

Cherry blossoms frame the Jefferson Memorial

V. Annual Festivals in Washington, D.C.

Arguably the most enticing time of the year to photograph in Washington, D.C., is during the National Cherry Blossom Festival, which occurs in late March and early April. But major holidays provide other wonderful photo ops.

National Cherry Blossom Festival (25)

Early each spring, the best justification for being in Washington, D.C., having absolutely nothing to do with politics is the blossoming of some three thousand cherry trees. The trees were a gift from Japan, beginning in 1912, commemorating the 1854 Treaty of Peace and Amity, officially establishing formal relations between the two nations.

Photographing the cherry blossoms during the festival immerses you in a dramatic moment in the annual cycle of nature in our nation's capital. Your timing for photos of maximum blossoms is critical, and it depends on the cycle of moisture, cold, and heat that triggers the white Yoshino and pink Akebono blossoms. The blossoms are so delicate and so temporary. The blooming usually occurs during the last days of March or the first days of April, so check with the city's tourism information source (www.washington.org) to make sure you will be photographing on peak days. Expect that everyone around you will be in a euphoric mood.

The area of greatest concentration of these trees is around the Tidal Basin. To get the best shots, you'll want to walk around the Tidal Basin on a glorious, sunny day. A morning walk and an afternoon walk will present changing perspectives.

Keep in mind two important aspects of your cherry blossom adventure:

• Transportation will be an issue. Think twice before trying to bring a car to the Tidal Basin, especially on a weekend. Rather, park elsewhere, and come in by taxi or on the Metro, getting off at the Smithsonian station, about a 10-minute walk from the Tidal Basin.

• Prepare yourself for possibly chilly weather. Even on sunny days, the wind can be brisk in April. Keep in mind that you will be walking for some distance. Make it a fun outing with food and drink in a daypack. Pausing to linger meditatively amid the cherry blossoms is a major pleasure. Portable toilets are scattered throughout the area should you not wish to leave the vicinity if nature calls.

Start where Maine Avenue meets the Kutz Bridge. Walk toward the Tidal Basin water from that intersection, and begin photographing. Here are the classic shots:

Walking southeast along the Tidal Basin puts you amid the cherry trees in all their abundance, with the Thomas Jefferson Memorial across the water. Frame the Jefferson Memorial with cherry blossoms. The light will change throughout the day, so your opportunities for beautiful photos will also evolve. Consider shooting at 10 A.M. and returning at 4 P.M. to get entirely different sun angles.

Another concept is a close-up of a cherry blossom twig set against the blue sky. You can do this with your telephoto lens focused on a blossom cluster.

Continue to walk southeast along the Tidal Basin all the way around to the Jefferson Memorial, keeping the lovely cherry trees and the Jefferson Memorial in front of you. But also look back. Consider a photo framing the Washington Monument in cherry blossoms. Some exceptional shots are possible when you look back from this angle. This is an important general truth when photographing this city: You may focus on a wide-angle close-up of a scene immediately in front of you, and then glance around and find that another icon appears in the distance, worthy of a zoom-in photo.

Walk all the way to the Jefferson Memorial, and spend some time enjoying and photographing it, as is discussed in Chapter I.

To further enhance your Cherry Blossom Festival experience, attend the **Cherry Blossom Parade** on Constitution Avenue. This event is an extraordinary display of Americana, with military marching bands and high school units of many kinds. Consider photographing patriotic groups in the Cherry Blossom parade. There are also units dressed in historic costumes. You may find a colonial America drum and fife corps in costume. For the exact date of the parade, visit www.washington.org.

There is also a **Japanese Cherry Blossom Street Festival,** known as Sakura Matsuri, on Freedom Square near the White House. Wander the scene and consider photographing the food stalls or the performance venues. For example, you might see a martial arts performance with the Capitol building in the background.

For all these good photo opportunities and celebratory life experiences, the Cherry Blossom Festival ranks as a memorable spring event to put on your calendar.

July Fourth Fireworks (26)

The July Fourth fireworks on the National Mall is another major occasion at which to take

July Fourth fireworks light up the Washington sky

July Fourth fireworks as seen from Arlington, Virginia

striking photographs. When fireworks burst over the Washington Monument or the Capitol, the image can be a stirring celebration of patriotism in America.

A considerable amount of strategic planning is required to get good fireworks shots. The first question is: Where should you be located? The two main options—giving an equally pleasing view—are along the Mall itself or over in Virginia, either on the hillside at the Netherlands Carillon near the Iwo Jima Memorial or at some private venue in Arlington such as Top

of the Town. From the Mall you can get a wide-angle image of the Washington Monument with bursts of fireworks around it. From the Virginia side you can get a compressed long-lens view of fireworks with the icons in the photo.

Be aware that you will not be alone. People will arrive early, stake out a territory, bring their picnics and beverages of choice (though alcohol is technically forbidden on public land), jostle for position, and settle in. This is one time when the restriction on tripods tends to be relaxed. Try to scout out your vantage point in advance. Be aware of your location and the potential bad behavior of other people. Especially on the Mall, you'll need to make some early decisions and live with them.

If people begin standing up in front of your camera during the fireworks, you won't get any good shots. If you're on the Mall, for example, you might want to position yourself along the Reflecting Pool so no obtuse reveler could stand in front of you. The hillside at the Netherlands Carillon is more forgiving. It's unlikely that someone will get in your line of sight as you position in your viewfinder the Washington Monument, Capitol Building, and Lincoln Memorial with fireworks exploding overhead.

If you haven't photographed fireworks before, a few technical details need to be learned. First, you'll need a sturdy tripod. (A tripod will be allowed in the middle of the Mall and at the Iwo Jima Memorial.) Second, photos with several bursts of fireworks in one shot are often better than just one. You may want to set your camera in manual mode, with your ISO to 100, your aperture at f/11, and then open the shutter on "bulb" with a cabled shutter release. First shoot a photo of your background components, such as the Washington Monument, and count how long it takes the camera to record the image suitably—not too dark and not too blasted out. Look at your display on the back of the camera to read this appropriate exposure. Suppose it's about two seconds to get the background right. Now the fireworks are starting to shoot off. By holding open the shutter, you'll allow the bursts of fireworks to "paint" the black sky. With a piece of dark cardboard or a black plastic CD case at the ready, you can open your camera exposure, catch a burst, and then slide the visual barrier in front of the lens. If you want a total of two seconds of exposure, you could catch three bursts at a little less than one second each by using the black barrier. Try to do several photos with different numbers of bursts to see what pleases you. You'll have to work quickly. The 2008 fireworks lasted 17 minutes. Your clearest shots might be your first efforts because smoke can sometimes obscure later images.

If you can, do a "practice run" at some local festival and become familiar in general with night shooting (see Chapter VI). Nothing is more frustrating than getting all set up, only to learn that you have a technical challenge and aren't getting good images. If you come to Washington's grand fireworks display after having already experimented, you're more likely to get good photo results.

Christmas in D.C. (27)

Christmas is a festive time in Washington, D.C. One essential icon to photograph is the **National Christmas Tree**—a live tree planted immediately south of the White House on the Ellipse. The large tree is adorned with ample decorations, complete with an entire Victorian gingerbread village and toy train at its base. With a wide-angle lens, it's possible to get a photo of all three elements: the tree, the village, and the White House in the distant background. The photo works well on sunny, clear-sky days from noon to perhaps 3 in the afternoon, when the low-hanging winter sun shines in the southern and western sky, illuminating all the elements. Security guards probably won't permit you to use a tripod, either day or night, so it's difficult to do a successful night shot of the tree. And note that the tree decorations are removed promptly a few days after Christmas, so be sure to get there in a timely manner.

Another well-lit tree stands in front of the **Capitol** on the sweeping lawns west of the building. An afternoon photo with the sun illuminating the tree and the Capitol works well. The setting of the Capitol tree is particularly congenial if snow covers the ground—and people haven't tracked in the snow to ruin the

The National Christmas Tree at the White House

shops, is decorated in a Christmas theme, with lit trees, poinsettias, and other finery. This is a good time to photograph the great dome of the building from its interior with some Christmas decor in the image.

Cultural Festivals on the National Mall (28)

A year-round cycle of festivals and citizen use enlivens the Mall, presenting many good photo opportunities. For specific information about what's going on during your visit, visit www.washington.org. One especially fun example is a **Kite Festival**, held on the last Saturday in March.

One of the best opportunities to take interesting people photos on the Mall is the annual **Smithsonian Folklife Festival**. Taking place for two weeks in late June and early July to overlap the Fourth of July holiday, this elaborate event put on by the Smithsonian Institution's Center for Folklife and Cultural Heritage celebrates contemporary cultural traditions. Each year various traditions are celebrated in programs that feature a particular nation, region, state, or theme. In 2008 the Kingdom of Bhutan, Texas and the Deep South, and NASA (for the 50th anniversary of the National Aeronautics and Space Administration) were highlighted. Regardless of which part of the world is featured on any given year, expect to find much camera-worthy subject matter such as music, song, worship, dance, crafts, cooking, storytelling, and workers' culture at this diversified multiday event. Full details can be found at www.folklife.si.edu.

The Mall is truly a commons for the people. Aside from special festivals and events, on a summer night you might find a dozen softball teams competing within sight of the Washington Monument—or people just strolling and enjoying a lovely evening. More can be learned about the National Mall at www.nps.gov/nama.

Washington, D.C., so you need to get lucky in winter or be prepared to arrive on short notice for snow shots. Again, tripods are generally not allowed at the Capitol.

Union Station, the great rail terminus, is quite festive year-round but especially so at Christmas. The interior of the building, always lively with people enjoying its restaurants and

Bhutanese monks participate in the annual Smithsonian Folklife Festival on the Mall

The illuminated Washington Monument and the Reflecting Pool

VI. Night Light on the Icons

Photos at night are some of the most exciting aesthetic possibilities in D.C., especially along the National Mall with its iconic buildings, monument, and memorials. As mentioned in the Introduction, respect the tripod restrictions by not attempting to use a tripod at the White House, on the Capitol grounds, and in high-traffic places such as the close-in parts of the Lincoln Memorial. The White House is moderately well lit at night, but you will need a beanbag or a high ISO for effective shots. The other icons are well lit and have plenty of tripod-friendly space around them for you to get your shots.

Night is a pleasing, tranquil, and quiet time to photograph on the Mall. Gone are the hustle, bustle, and noise of the day. Night shooting brings out the meditative side of the city and a reflective pause amid the crushing burdens of governance, with all its partisan wrangling.

If you have a car, you can park it alongside the Potomac River adjacent to the Memorial Bridge. Parking is not difficult at night. However, the walk to the Mall is a quarter mile or so.

One of the photographic joys of the Mall is its Reflecting Pool and also the large water pool in front of the Capitol. These watery surfaces allow for reflective images that can be intriguing both night and day—but they're especially haunting at night.

Night at the Washington Monument (29)

Go to the Reflecting Pool at the base of the Lincoln Memorial and capture a vertical of the Washington Monument and its reflection in the water. Get there a half hour before darkness, when there's still some ambient light in the sky. Compare your results both with fading light and with total black sky to see what pleases you. Horizontal and vertical compositions are equally possible. For the horizontal, carefully watch your position, locate yourself directly in the center at the end of the Reflecting Pool, double-check in your viewfinder that your horizon is level, and balance out the trees on either side. You'll want to have a fairly wide-angle lens as well as a long lens plus as sturdy a tripod as possible to hold your camera in position. A cabled shutter release will allow you to avoid camera shake when you trip the shutter. At 100 or 200 ISO and f/8, your camera may take a few seconds to gauge the appropriate light.

Night at the Lincoln Memorial (30)

When you're finished with your Washington Monument shoot, walk around the security barriers and into the Lincoln Memorial, and position your tripod-mounted camera at the bottom of the steps. This is as close in as you should try to get with a tripod, even at night, because of the crowds. Test your luck with a tripod closer in if you wish, but be prepared that a guard might restrict you. From this flat area near the barrier, you can make a wide-angle shot of the entire Lincoln Memorial.

However, another interesting night photo here is a telephoto close-up of the seated Lincoln with silhouetted people standing in front of him. The photo suggests Lincoln's prominence. People come to see him day and night. This is possibly the busiest people-traffic area in D.C.

Night at the Capitol (31)

When you're done at the Mall, head back to your car (or catch a taxi), and drive to the

The illuminated Abraham Lincoln and nighttime visitors

Capitol. It's easy to park at night on the north side of the large pool in front of the building. Don't try to go in close with a tripod on the Capitol grounds. You'll find out as we have that an armed guard on a bicycle will probably confront you and warn, "No tripods!" Photos just as effective can be made with your tripod and the right lenses from across the pool in front of the Capitol. Walk along this pool to find gaps in the trees that give you a clean shot of the Capitol. Then, with a long lens, you can get a close-up of the Capitol dome at night. With a wide-angle lens, you can take lovely photos of the dome and its reflection in the water.

Chances are, if you make some efforts with night shots, you'll come away with images that will please you. (Note: For night shots with the July Fourth fireworks, see Chapter V.)

The Capitol and its reflection

John and Jacqueline Kennedy's house in Georgetown during his Senate years

VII. Neighborhoods

Photographing the neighborhoods of Washington, D.C., can be fun—especially if you like to walk and experience the serendipity of a city. Three neighborhoods are especially intriguing.

Georgetown

Georgetown is a historic and fashionable district of low-rise brick townhouses, now protected by architectural controls. Originally a trading town before there was a concept of the federal city known as Washington, D.C., the area's name was a tribute to King George II, not George Washington.

Walk **M Street NW between 28th and 34th Streets NW (32)** to get started on this neighborhood photographic foray. The heart of the area is Wisconsin Avenue NW and M Street NW.

Tour the side streets to see the old-money mansions. Two of these have JFK associations. In the 1950s, during his Senatorial career, John F. and Jacqueline Kennedy lived at **Marbury House (33)**, 3307 N Street NW. After JFK's assassination, his widow resided at **3017 N Street NW (34)**. Both these facades face south, so they are in good light for photos for much of the day. There can be seasonal touches to enhance a photo, such as a dogwood in bloom in April at 3307 N Street NW.

Georgetown is the start of the historic **Chesapeake and Ohio (C&O) Canal (35)**, which offers many seasonal photo opportunities as well as hiking and biking along its towpath. Running 184.5 miles from Washington, D.C., to Cumberland, Maryland, this historic canal once brought in goods from the West to what was the Port of Georgetown. (For further details, see Chapter IX.) To make an image of

Jogging along the historic C&O Canal in Georgetown

one of D.C.'s oldest surviving structures, seek out the **Old Stone House (36)**, as it is affectionately known, at 3051 M Street NW. This lovely stone structure, still extant amid the hustle and

Built in 1765, the Old Stone House is the city's oldest standing structure

Dumbarton Oaks (37), a historic plantation house, 31st and R Streets NW, offers 10 acres of tranquil outdoor gardens, with many photographic possibilities of astute garden design and intimate rest spots. (Note, however, that commercial photography is not permit-

bustle of shops, was built in 1765 by a carpenter named Christopher Layman. The park service now manages it as a portrait of life in the 18th century. The Old Stone House is located on a busy street, so it's difficult to shoot a photo without an obstructing car parked in front of it. Use an extremely wide-angle lens from the corner of the house to get a strong vertical image. The house faces south, so it has good light on it throughout the day.

ted.) The mansion houses the Dumbarton Oaks Research Library and Collection, a center for scholarship in Byzantine studies, Pre-Columbian studies, and the history of landscape architecture, so the house is now a showcase of specialized and exquisite art objects, which can be photographed if you don't use a flash. The first-rate Byzantine and Mexican pieces, among others, are well lit and well displayed, so they can be successfully photographed with a handheld digital camera. The front of the mansion faces south, giving it good

The stately 1801 Federal-style Dumbarton Oaks is now a research library and museum

light on it for much of the day. For hours and additional information, see www.doaks.org. Although picnicking isn't permitted on the grounds, nearby **Montrose Park (38)** offers an ideal place for a cheerful alfresco lunch. Located at the north end of Georgetown along R Street, between Dumbarton Oaks and Oak Hill Cemetery, the park is a popular outdoor destination for Georgetown residents. Look for the boxwood maze, Lovers Lane, and a handsome cobblestone walkway on the west side of the park.

Wander the back streets of Georgetown, between M and R Streets NW, from 28th to 34th Streets NW, and you'll find many photogenic **brick houses (39)**. The setting is particularly congenial in April, when azaleas and dogwoods are in bloom.

Dupont Circle

Dupont Circle has a certain cachet, home to the young, hip Washington intelligentsia. You'll feel the aura of the scene as you walk, photograph, and people-watch.

Start at the **Dupont Circle Metro (40)** exit and look around. Admire the fountain, the urban greenery, and the young elite who live here. Something fun is often taking place at the Circle. On our last visit, we listened to a gifted ensemble of young wind instrumentalists, mainly trombonists, calling themselves The Kings of Harmony. They were from a local church and were blowing such mellow notes that a half dozen observers begged to buy a CD. This was a wonderful serendipitous example of what, as a photographer in D.C, you just might stumble upon.

Wind ensemble entertaining passersby at Dupont Circle

The Indonesian Embassy on Massachusetts Avenue NW—part of Embassy Row

One walk (or drive, since the distances are not short) could take you west of Dupont Circle up Massachusetts Avenue—the start of **Embassy Row (41)**—to Sheridan Circle and beyond. There are many interesting structures to photograph along Embassy Row, such as the **Indonesian Embassy (42)** at 2020 Massachusetts Avenue NW. This was formerly the **Walsh-McLean House**, said to be the poshest house in Washington when it was built in 1903.

The Islamic Center for Washington, D.C. (43), at 2551 Massachusetts Avenue NW, has distinctive and recognizable mosque architecture suggestive of the Islamic world. Several Muslim nations have their embassies nearby.

Special photo opportunities of embassy interiors are possible in May, during an open house called **Passport DC**. Time your visit right, and you may be able to experience and photograph native dancing, food, and cultural programs.

If you don't mind a vigorous walk, consider turning right at Belmont Street NW, then right on Kalorama, and return to the Metro

The Islamic Center on Embassy Row

The French ambassador's residence on Kalorama Street

via Connecticut. This will take you past the **French ambassador's house (44)** at 2221 Kalorama Road NW, one of area's grandest residences. You can photograph the house through an iron fence. The sun hits this south-facing house for much of the day.

Another, shorter walk takes you up Connecticut Avenue a few blocks to Kalorama Road. Turn right on Kalorama to enjoy a quiet street with stone mansions of the wealthy.

You could keep ambling beyond Kalorama to 18th Street and the Adams-Morgan district. There is a random delight involved in walking the area. We remember the day we stumbled on the **colorful row houses (45)** at Seaton Place

and 17th Street NW—a charming street of narrow colonial houses with colorful facades that make for great photos.

Adams-Morgan

If you want to photograph an ethnically and culturally diverse neighborhood, Adams-Morgan would be an excellent choice, starting at 18th Street NW and Columbia Road NW. An energetic Latino and African community flourishes here, with many other cultural heritages also represented. The African community is especially robust, with new immigrants as well as a slave legacy going back to the Civil War. Jazz great Duke Ellington flourished here

Mural for Madam's Organ restaurant in the Adams-Morgan district

as a child. Today the music, nightlife, and restaurant scene thrives. (If you want to pause for an ethnic meal after your shoot, consider the Ethiopian restaurant **Meskerem**, 2434 18th Street NW.)

Mural Art (46)

The Adams-Morgan neighborhood is justly famous for its mural art—all colorful subjects for photos. The oldest of these murals is **Un Pueblo Sin Murales** at 1779 Columbia Road NW. This 1970s creation is a complex politi-

cal statement, painted by two Chilean immigrant artists who fled the repressive Pinochet regime.

Next, walk down 18th Street NW to view the two most famous murals, the risqué bare-breasted **Madam's Organ** mural, 2461 18th Street NW, on the outside of a blues and bluegrass club of the same name. The same block, at 2461 18th Street NW, has the famous painting by Parisian artist **Toulouse-Lautrec** of cabaret singer **Artistide Bruant** replicated on the outside of a building.

These three murals are symbols of the political edginess, creative energy, and irreverence typical of the Adams-Morgan district. You might want to check out the list of additional murals in the Adams-Morgan section at www.culturaltourismdc.org. This irreverent artwork has become the visual signature of the Adams-Morgan area—about as famous as the mural of **Marilyn Monroe** at **Calvert Street and Connecticut Avenue** in the nearby Woodley Park neighborhood.

Adams-Morgan Heritage Trail Walk (47)

To enhance your visit to Adams-Morgan, consider walking the Adams-Morgan Heritage Trail, called **Roads to Diversity**. Start at Florida Avenue NW and 16th Street, and you'll see the first of 18 poster-size guides to the cultural heritage of the area. The Meridian Hill marker will explain how the unusual park, with its lavish fountains, was created. You'll learn how the Union Army hospital and camp on Meridian Hill first attracted African American freedom seekers to the area. By 1910 Mexico, Ecuador, Cuba, and Spain all had embassies clustered on 16th Street NW.

When you walk the trail, the poster presentations will illuminate the subjects you find visually interesting. If you want to prepare in advance for your photo shoot, you can download an entire trail booklet by going to www.culturaltourismdc.org and clicking on the Adams-Morgan section.

Kalorama Park (48)

For people photos in the Adams-Morgan district, one place to hang out is Kalorama Park, a 3-acre triangular park located at the intersection of Columbia Road, Kalorama Road, and 19th Street NW. A parade of locals will pass before you in this park, with its shade trees, tennis courts, and recreation center. One special aspect of the park is the community garden, whose ample-sized gardening plots are chosen by lottery every five years. Here you can photograph the modern urban food-growing movement as citizens tend their plants. The word *Kalorama,* Greek for "beautiful view," was originally the name of an estate in the area. Capture the beauty of the park and the cultural richness of Adams-Morgan in your photos.

Colorful row houses enliven the Dupont Circle neighborhood

The lobby of the historic Willard Hotel

VIII. Landmark Hotels, Railways, and Notable Markets

Since Washington, D.C., is a major world capital, you would expect to find prominent hotels, railway stations, and shopping in this city. They are also interesting to look at and photograph.

Landmark Hotels

W Washington (49)

Located a block from the White House at 515 15th Street NW, the former **Hotel Washington** has been completely renovated—including a name change. But the hotel has preserved the historic rooftop garden, which in summer allows you a bird's-eye view of many of the memorials. During the chill of winter there is an adjacent ice-skating rink. The W, as it's known, also offers the visitor an opportunity to gaze down at civil servants doing our bidding at the **U.S. Treasury Building**, a mock-Greek columned edifice like so much Washington architecture. As a humorist once observed, "The Treasury is the one place they can print money faster than we can spend it."

Willard Hotel (50)

The Willard, 1401 Pennsylvania Avenue NW, dates from 1901, but a hotel has stood on the site since 1816, and Abraham Lincoln is said to have stayed there. The Willard was where Martin Luther King prepared his "I Have a Dream" speech in 1963. As you photograph the ornate wood-paneled lobby of the Willard, you might note that the word "lobbyist" is said to have originated right here, coined for the powerful and influential persons who hung around in the hotel lobby trying to sway the politicians as they came and went.

Railways

Union Station is one of the country's major rail terminals. The Metro is likely to become your friend in Washington since it's *the* efficient way to get around. Interesting photo opportunities await at both.

Union Station (51)

Walking through its cavernous lobby of Union Station (50 Massachusetts Avenue NE) reminds one of the day when the train was virtually the only way to get to Washington. The historic large main hall and adjacent levels host a diverse dining and shopping scene, with more than 120 shops. To define the essence of this 1908 beaux arts masterpiece in one photo, position yourself near the information booth, and capture the great vaulted ceiling of the main hall, also called the **Grand Concourse**.

Mount the stairs to the main restaurant in the Grand Concourse, the **Center Café**. This places you at a high point in the main hall. Walk around this circular elevated site, and take photos of the scene. A wide-angle lens can capture the glorious vaulted ceiling and the many people scurrying to and fro, entering or leaving the nation's capital by rail.

The Metro (52)

One unusual aspect of the Metro is how deep it is underground, making the escalators remarkable in their length. Photograph the **escalator at Dupont Circle** as one of the longest escalator rides you will ever experience as well as an interesting graphic. Generally, though, as a photograph in and of itself, the Metro presents a gray and cavelike appearance. Most of

The vaulted ceiling of famed Union Station

what is of interest for photography in the city is within a brisk walk of the Metro. Learn to use the Metro efficiently and you will save yourself a lot of time. Distances can be deceiving in Washington. Edifices such as the Washington Monument and the Capitol Building are so large that you may think you can walk there in a few minutes. But they may actually be a couple of miles away.

Metro escalator at Dupont Circle

Plus, in D.C. surface travel during rush hour may come to a total standstill. We have sat for an hour in auto gridlock at 6 P.M. on the streets west of the White House to travel just a few blocks from Adams-Morgan down to the National Mall. The Metro keeps running while there may a standstill overhead.

Shopping for African textiles at Eastern Market

Notable Markets

Photographing the outdoor markets of a vibrant city can be quite rewarding, and Washington is no exception—from its main fish market to its farmers' markets, whether occasional or permanent.

Maine Avenue Fish Market (53)

The sumptuous seafood market known as the Maine Avenue Fish Market (1100 Maine Avenue SW) provides an opportunity to photograph and enjoy the bounty of the Chesapeake Bay and nearby Atlantic Ocean. Here you can find the fabled blue crabs of the Chesapeake, alive or cooked, as well as an assortment of fresh ocean fish, including red snapper and rockfish. If your lodging situation in D.C. includes a kitchen, this is the place to stock up after a day of exploring and shooting the capital before you return to your digs to prepare a gourmet feast.

Eastern Market (54)

Farmers' markets as well as outdoor crafts markets can be intriguing places to photograph. One of our favorites is Eastern Market at 7th Street and North Carolina Avenue SE, east of the Capitol in one of the oldest residential areas in the city. This daily market has a huge diversity of fresh fish, meat, and produce, but Saturday is the liveliest day because of the large outdoor flea market, with exotic wares such as African textiles in a stall called the Great Zimbabwe.

Only a short walk east from the Capitol, Eastern Market is thriving, and the neighborhood, once chancy, is now flourishing, with the historic brick homes appreciating in value. The best time for a photographic visit would be on a Saturday, when both the farmers' market and the flea market are in operation.

IX. "Natural" Washington, D.C.

Nature's display in Washington offers more opportunities for photography and enjoyment than might be assumed. Two singular natural events are subjects in themselves: the Cherry Blossom Festival in spring (see Chapter V) and the fall colors of October (see Chapter X). But ample parkland within the city entices visitors and residents alike with miles of trails for hiking and photographing. The **Rock Creek Parkway**, for example, has the feel of a pristine, mountain roadway.

Three major venues in Washington itself and in the region are especially worthy of your photographic attention.

Theodore Roosevelt Island (55)

This rustic 91-acre wooded island in the Potomac, with its 1.3-mile walking path and natural vegetation, will surprise a typical Washington visitor. Though you are in the middle of one of the great urban centers of the world, this island preserve a few miles from the White House is like a wilderness. As an antidote—or perhaps a counterpoint—to the urban scene, Theodore Roosevelt Island is one of our favorite places, offering a tranquility that political partisanship cannot intrude upon. Even a birder may get a few credible photos with a long lens.

Taking nature photos here is a fitting tribute to our 26th president, who spent much of his political capital on efforts to preserve the outdoors at a period when America's natural resources were, for the first time, seen as exhaustible. Roosevelt provided public protection for nearly 230 million acres of land in the United States during his presidency, using a spectrum of political arrangements such as national parks, forests, monuments, bird reservations, and game reserves.

Hiking path on Theodore Roosevelt Island

Look at the map before planning your outing. You'll need to drive (or take a cab) to get here. From D.C., cross the Theodore Roosevelt Memorial Bridge, and head northwest on the George Washington Memorial Parkway to a small parking lot. Minimal signage alerts you to the parking lot. You then walk across a pedestrian bridge to the island.

As you walk around the island, enjoying this densely wooded, green environment, note a **statue of Roosevelt**. A blustery populist icon, this man known as the Rough Rider was equally at home in Washington as he was on the Dakota Badlands and in the Amazon.

The walk is most pleasing and especially lovely to photograph in April and May, when there is a torrid burst of green growth in the deciduous trees and the understory bushes. There are many opportunities to photograph hikers, bikers, nature lovers, and dog enthusiasts, who like this dog-friendly area. Morning from 8 to 10 is a good time, when the light is soft and angled. For more information about Theodore Roosevelt Island, go to www.nps.gov/this.

Hike/Bike/Cruise the C&O Canal (56)

Starting in Georgetown—descending to it from the Francis Scott Key Bridge area—the Chesapeake & Ohio Canal is another lovely, rustic aspect of Washington, D.C., that you can access at any time of year. The canal extends 185 miles upriver to Cumberland, in western Maryland.

While in Georgetown, stop in at the National Park Service office for the C&O Canal in back of the house at 1057 Jefferson Street NW. For their hours, check out the Web site at www.nps.gov/choh. The park service visitors center is useful for maps and information. A picturesque canal barge, the *Georgetown*, leaves from there for two-hour narrated excursions,

Cycling along the C&O Canal

The **Charles F. Mercer** *on the C&O Canal at Great Falls*

April to October. A lock and the *Georgetown* make for a compelling photo.

In spring and summer the C&O bursts with new green growth; in autumn it displays a warm fall color palette. The water, the trees, and the people along the pathway can all be part of your photo compositions.

Take a walk or ride a bike along this famous towpath where mules once pulled barges. (Bike rentals are possible in Georgetown from **Big Wheel Bikes**, 1034 33rd Street NW.) Signage and legacy equipment along the waterway will alert you to the history. Started in 1828 as the "Great National Project," it took 22 years for the excavators to get to Cumberland, Maryland, which fell short of the dream to dig the canal all the way to Pittsburgh on the Ohio River. From 1850 to 1924 the canal flourished as a watery highway. The main raw material shipped downriver to D.C. was coal, but corn,

wheat, and lumber were also substantial commodities. However, a rival technology, the railroad, was competing for shipping business, and the Baltimore and Ohio Railroad actually reached Cumberland before the canal. Although the canal was doomed by the developing rail option, the C&O Canal was still a major and ingenious element of commerce, floating goods on dependable, level water.

Great Falls Park (57)

Besides the option of starting your canal excursion in Georgetown, consider also beginning farther out, 14.5 miles upriver from Georgetown. Great Falls Park is, arguably, the finest nature experience available in the D.C. area. It's a pleasant drive out along the **Clara Barton Parkway**, which honors the founder of the American Red Cross. Numerous stops provide access to the trail and canal, notably at locks 6,

7, 8, and 10, though you need to drive beyond them and backtrack for a stop, due to the narrow roads. Memorable views of the forest and canal abound in all seasons.

On entering the park, be sure to ask for the two National Park Service brochures, *Hiking Trails of Great Falls, Maryland* and *Chesapeake and Ohio Canal*. The latter can be seen online at www.nps.gov/choh. If you have time to photograph just one nature site in the Washington, D.C., region, Great Falls Park would be our recommendation.

At Great Falls, the former Great Falls Tavern is now a park interpretive center. Walk out along the elaborate boardwalks to the **Great Falls Overlook**, and experience the dramatic, crashing force of the Potomac River—something that could never be imagined from its docile appearance in D.C. proper. The existence of such treacherous falls necessitated building a secure water highway: the C&O Canal. Morning light is ideal for photos of the falls.

Also at Great Falls, the *Charles F. Mercer,* a canal boat pulled by mules, can take you on an excursion through a lock and along the towpath. The canal boat in operation with the mules makes an interesting historic-restoration photo.

Chesapeake Bay from Annapolis (58)

The water environment associated with Washington, D.C., mainly involving sprawling Chesapeake Bay, is one of the major aspects of the region to appreciate and photograph. We suggest taking a side trip to Annapolis, Maryland, east and north of the capital. The **U.S. Naval Academy** and the dining/art/cultural scene—including the state capitol—are additional subjects to photograph and experience. A Three Centuries Walking Tour leaves at 10:30 each morning from the visitors center (for further information, visit www.visitannapolis.org) at 26 West Street, taking you to historical build-

ings to photograph. Be sure to have a picture ID with you if you want to walk on U.S. Naval Academy grounds.

We especially like launching out into the Chesapeake Bay from the foot of City Dock via the one-hour narrated cruises by **Watermark Cruises**, offered April to September. One be-

Sailboats catch the wind on Chesapeake Bay off Annapolis

comes aware of the sailing culture, the naval war college, and the vast expanse of the waterway. It's also comforting to know that a few blue crabs are creating the next generation of culinary offerings on the bottom.

Sailboats on the bay are interesting to photograph, sometimes with a long lens and some-times wide-angle, depending on how close you are to them and how expansively you might want to include the sky. If you want to take photos of the sailboats in the harbor, walk over to the **Spa Creek Bridge** and beyond to **Back Creek**, where thousands of yachts and sailboats are moored.

Early fall colors reflect in the C&O Canal in Georgetown

X. Seasonal Washington, D.C.: Beyond the Cherry Blossom Festival

Seasonal D.C. will delight the traveler who aims a camera at spring and autumn. Summer can be hot, with leaden humidity, and winter can be dreary and spare—not such inviting times to photograph.

Of course, the Cherry Blossom Festival in early April is in a class by itself (see Chapter V). This annual display around the Tidal Basin is so beautiful as to bring tears to the observer. The great poet T. S. Eliot, in perhaps his most famous line, said, "April is the cruelest month." This blossoming of cherry trees will remind a photographer about the fragility of life and about mortality.

Late-Spring Flora and Fauna (59)

Shortly after cherry blossom time, throughout April and early May, there is a surge in fresh spring greenery, the full leafing out of trees, along with an outpouring of flowers. All this natural beauty makes metro Washington a delight to photograph. Of course, the two great nature areas, **Theodore Roosevelt Island** (site 55) and the **C&O Canal** (site 56), would be good locations to focus on, but there are also major floral displays within the city.

Prime tulip time unfortunately passes quickly—only from perhaps April 10 to April 20—so you'll need to time your visit carefully if you want to capture these flowers at their peak. The front of the **National Cathedral**, Massachusetts and Wisconsin Avenues NW, bursts with daffodils and tulips. The western, grassy side of the **Capitol** (site 3) and many planting areas around the various **Smithsonian** buildings display a lavish number of tulips. Plantings of tulips along the **National Mall** (site 7) can also be showy. There is a dense planting behind the Smithsonian's **Castle** headquarters (site 13). If you get down low, with a wide-angle lens, you can make appealing photos of the flowers with the specific building in the background. Capture the image with a small aperture, such as f/11, to insure that the entire length of the picture—from the flowers to the building—is in focus.

After the tulips fade, azaleas and dogwood bloom throughout the Washington, D.C., region, making springtime colorful and festive.

Late spring, before the onset of summer heat, is also an inviting time to explore and photograph the **National Zoo**. You will see the animals, such as the famous pandas, displayed with pleasing greenery in their natural-looking enclosures.

Fall Color (60)

The D.C. region is a glorious fall-color environment—something to savor in late October. Fall color can be seen only a stone's throw from the White House. Go to 17th and E Streets NW, and you'll see a brilliant maple tree with the **Washington Monument** (site 2) in the background.

Once again, this is a reminder that the icons of this city are so subtle to photograph in their year-round visual diversity. Try to frame each monument and memorial in its seasonal costume. The Washington Monument can be framed with cherry blossoms in spring or fall foliage in autumn. Every citizen who comes to Washington, D.C., on an autumn pilgrimage will enjoy the fiery presentation. Two glorious species of maple trees create the fall color. The

Tulips in their finery in front of the Capitol

red maple has leaves that turn purple. The sugar maple leaves appear to explode into flames.

You'll see this fall color on the **National Mall** (site 7), as mentioned, and also on the **George Washington Parkway** and the **Rock Creek Parkway**, if you're driving, and on hikes or bike trips on the **C&O Canal** (sites 35 and 56). And definitively put **Theodore Roosevelt Island** (site 55) on your fall-color-shot list. If you have the time, ability, and inclination to venture to the nearby Virginia countryside, excellent fall color shooting is possible at **Prince William Forest Park**.

After fall color fades, winter can set in fast in Washington, D.C., and the area has a severe and bleak look. The trees will be bare. Sometimes there will be fleeting snow on the ground, but this is an anomaly. More likely, the color palette will be gray skies and brown ground, with people hunkering down, waiting for spring. Earmuffs on the guard soldiers at the Tomb of the Unknown Soldier tell the story. In winter, all of Washington waits for the arrival of the spring season.

However, the spare form of winter trees can also have an interesting aesthetic appeal. The stark branches of trees before the I. M. Pei–designed **East Wing of the National Galley** (site 20) give the building a severe winter view that has appealing simplicity. The memorials to war, especially the **Korean War Veterans Memorial** (site 12), are sobering and severe in the chill of winter. The platoon of soldiers in the memorial marches across a winter field, seemingly suffering both from the cold and the strain of war.

The U.S. Air Force Memorial conjures up jet contrails

XI. Across the River from Washington, D.C.

The nearby Virginia region adjacent to Washington, D.C., is an integral part of the D.C. experience, both culturally and photographically. Traveling there will deepen your knowledge of the capital, going back to the Civil War. You will also encounter the lively town of **Alexandria** as well as **Mount Vernon**, the home of the beloved founder of the Republic, George Washington.

Navigating the area is most efficient by car, but the Metro (Arlington Station) and Tourmobile can be used for **Arlington National Cemetery**. The Metro also has a stop in Alexandria (King Street Station).

Arlington National Cemetery

Iconic Arlington (61)

Arlington National Cemetery is a sobering place to experience, both as a citizen and as a photographer. Here the sacrifices in war for the benefit of the Republic become apparent, evidenced by the estimated 290,000 soldiers and their family members buried here. You can capture images of the rows of white crosses in a creative manner. The simple monument to JFK is equally moving: an eternal flame for the gifted president who died so young. Morning light is the best time for photos because the

Graves in Arlington National Cemetery of those who served their country

Graves of JFK and Jacqueline Kennedy in Arlington National Cemetery

cemetery is on a hill facing east. You can get there by car, by the Metro at the Arlington stop, and via the Tourmobile, which takes you there from the National Mall. Tourmobiles circulate around Arlington at 20-minute intervals, so it's easy to get on or off at will.

Three other sites, beyond the rows of stark white crosses, should be considered for photos. You can walk through the cemetery to these destinations or take the Tourmobile to get to the sites:

John F. Kennedy Gravesite (62)
JFK's grave lies just below Robert E. Lee's mansion, Arlington House. Morning light falls on the eternal flame advantageously for photos. John and Jacqueline Kennedy are both buried here, and **Robert F. Kennedy** is buried to the left, his grave marked with a wooden cross. Some of the inspiring words of the slain Kennedy brothers are inscribed in stone. Get low to the ground with a wide-angle lens and you can capture a horizontal photo of the Kennedy grave, the eternal flame, and Arlington House.

The Tomb of the Unknowns (63)
Also known as the Tomb of the Unknown Soldier—the resting place for the remains of unidentified soldiers from World Wars I and II and Korea—the Tomb of the Unknowns is a

poignant symbol to photograph, a reminder of the ultimate sacrifice of so many soldiers in so many wars. An honor guard marches continuously back and forth, revering the fallen dead. A changing of the guard occurs every half hour. The tomb will be somewhat backlit in the morning, due to the angle of the site, but an effective photo can be made if you position yourself on the right side of the viewer area, and zoom in to isolate the wreath (always present), the guard marching toward you, and the large tomb itself in the background.

Robert E. Lee Home (64)

The spite and cruelty of war are much in evidence as you look at Robert E. Lee's mansion, Arlington House, a columned architectural gem. Lee, one of the golden young men of Virginia and a son of the South, sided with the Confederacy in the Civil War struggle, which was both about slavery and states' rights. The victors in the struggle determined that Lee's plantation grounds would become a graveyard forever, with thousands of graves of the Union dead on his front lawn—making the homestead an uncongenial place for Lee and his family to live. There was, of course, reason for bitterness on both sides of the Civil War: More than 600,000 men gave their lives in the conflict, more than all who have died in all other U.S. wars to this day.

The best photos of Arlington House tend to be from below at the Kennedy burial site, at an angle, with the mansion crowning the hill of

Tomb of the Unknowns in Arlington National Cemetery

Arlington House, General Robert E. Lee's ancestral home

green grass. Also, when you're at the house, the front facade in morning light makes an effective photo, with your widest angle lens.

Military Memorials

A trio of memorial tributes to the military should also be considered for photos.

Women in Military Service for America Memorial (65)

This memorial devotes itself to the empowerment, pride, and appreciation of America's military women. Walk inside to see ground-level displays devoted to the role of women in the military since the Revolutionary War. Then walk around the upstairs terrace level to read the thoughts of many women military leaders that are etched in glass.

The U.S. Marine Corps Memorial/Iwo Jima Memorial (66)

Looking back to World War II and the historic struggle in the Pacific, the United States wrestled with Japan for five years after the surprise of Pearl Harbor. American forces slowly crept back across the Pacific to vanquish the Land of the Rising Sun. The most symbolic photo of this struggle—perhaps, indeed, of the entire war—was taken by Joseph Rosenthal in his image of soldiers raising an American flag on the island of Iwo Jima. At this Virginia site, that image is replicated in a 78-foot-long sculpture. Go to the U.S. Marine Corps War Memorial, more colloquially known as the Iwo Jima Memorial, to make your own image of this gargantuan battle.

The front of the image is a morning shot, with full light on it. Get down low with a wide-angle lens and a horizontal perspective to crop out the apartment buildings in the background. The sculpture can also be shot in afternoon light, from the back, alone or with the iconic structures of D.C. in the background. At night the sculpture is lit. Effective backlit shots at dawn are a further possibility.

The hillside near the sculpture also happens to be a premier place to get long-lens July Fourth shots of fireworks exploding over the icons (see Chapter V). The choice location is in front of the **Netherlands Carillon**, which celebrates the close ties between the Netherlands and the United States during the dark days of the German occupation.

U.S. Air Force Memorial (67)

The relatively new Air Force Memorial—it was dedicated in 2006—located near the Pentagon in Arlington, Virginia, is a striking subject for a photo. You'll need a car or cab to get there.

Take the Columbia Pike exit off Highway 395, and follow the signs to the memorial. Abundant parking exists in a designated lot opposite the entrance.

The United States Air Force Memorial honors the service and sacrifices of the men and women of the air force and its predecessor organizations. More than 54,000 airmen have died in combat.

An early-morning shot, looking up at the abstract elegance of this memorial, can be made from the sidewalk immediately below it, framing the image of three, curved stainless-steel towers. A dark-blue sky behind the sculpture will be ideal, enhancing the impression of three jets peeling off in formation or perhaps their contrails. Walking amid the sculpture, look up with your widest wide-angle lens to capture this lyrical and imaginative graphic, which is meant to evoke flight. Your task as a photographer will be to get in close and frame the sculpture with the sky, retaining its visual purity.

Iwo Jima sculpture at the U.S. Marine Corps Memorial

Historic King Street in Alexandria, Virginia

Old Alexandria

Historic Old Town (68)

Urban planners often talk about the "social capital" that helps or hinders a city to succeed, determining whether it is a fun place to live and work. Cities can decline, or they can become more vital. An interesting example to peruse and photograph in the D.C. region is downtown Alexandria, Virginia.

Alexandria began in 1699 as a port city, long before Washington, D.C., existed. Nowadays restaurants, shops, and art studios locate themselves in its historic houses and warehouses. A Metro stop, King Street, places you in the historic Old Town, which runs down King Street to the Potomac River and extends a block or two north and south. A free local trolley will transport you along King Street. Stop in at the Alexandria tourism office at 221 King Street for maps and brochures, or visit their Web site at www.visitalexandriava.com to orient yourself before a visit.

Outdoor dining, boutique shopping, historic buildings, and excursion boats for Potomac River trips attract visitors to Alexandria. A photographer can concentrate on a number of themes here.

Buildings with historic significance make intriguing photos, both exteriors and interiors. Here are three top contenders:

At the **Torpedo Factory Art Center (69)**, 105 North Union Street, World War I torpedoes were assembled. Today it houses artists and artisans. The compelling photo here is not the exterior of the building but rather what takes place inside on its three levels. Numerous residents are at work in their studios/shops, giving you ample opportunity to photograph artists and craftspeople in action.

The **Stabler-Leadbeater Apothecary Museum (70)**, 105-107 South Fairfax Street, captures the world of an 18th-century Quaker pharmacist, including a collection of lovely hand-blown bottles.

Gadsby's Tavern Museum (71), 134 North Royal Street, shows what a tavern at the time of George Washington and Thomas Jefferson looked like. Men of their stature spent a lot of time in such taverns, carrying on their businesses and talking politics. Washington liked to have his birthday parties in this tavern.

Nearby Virginia

George Washington's Home at Mount Vernon (72)

When you visit the region where the word "Washington" finds its way, with affection, into the name of the city, the large (and sole) "monument," the most beloved green parkway, and many other monikers, sooner or later you may want to photograph the home of this revered man and understand him a little better.

George Washington lived south of Alexandria at Mount Vernon. Head down from D.C. and Alexandria on the **George Washington Memorial Parkway**, and watch for the Mount Vernon signage.

The main photo to get is of the house itself, sitting on a hill above the Potomac, a regal plantation-style abode fitting for a golden son of Virginia. Facing east, the house and its columns, are a lovely early-morning shot. There is also good light in the afternoon for photos on the west side—the "front"—of the house. No photos are allowed inside, which is regrettable, since the house is a carefully restored 1799 snapshot of how it is presumed to have looked, based on a careful inventory taken at the time of Washington's death. The exquisite dining room, for example, shows Washington's artistic taste, including ceiling ornamental displays of his favorite farming crop, wheat.

Walk around the grounds, and numerous other photo ideas may intrigue you. The setting is both breathtaking and orderly, with the stately house sited so advantageously on a hill, the panoramic view of the waterway, the luxurious old hardwood trees, and the carefully laid-out and managed agricultural enterprises. The Hog Island sheep that Washington favored as a breed continue to be bred here. In summer the orchard trees will be laden with fruit. Flower, herb, and vegetable gardens are also re-created. Washington was an expert and innovative agriculturalist and a progressive

Stabler-Leadbeater Apothecary Museum in Alexandria

inventor in many matters. His favorite description of himself was "farmer." You can capture many photographic details of Washington's grand vision of an agriculture-based estate.

The drive down and back to Mount Vernon on the George Washington Memorial Parkway is one of the more pleasant road trips in the region. The parkway will help a photographer get closer to nature and to history. The drive unfolds in a wide swath of ongoing greenery with gracious curves and few stoplights, except for some in Alexandria. On the east side of the parkway, in the section from D.C. south to Mount Vernon, lies the Potomac and several parks that are good for a picnic or bike/hike access to the lovely trail running the full length of the parkway. **Belle Haven Park (73)** would be a good choice for a stop. There you can photograph bicyclists zooming along the parkway path as well as hardwood trees at the edge of the Potomac River. Known as the **Mount Vernon Trail**, the pathway winds 18.5 miles along the river from Mount Vernon to Theodore Roosevelt Island in D.C.

Another parkway stop near the capital offers an only-in-Washington photographic option. Turn off at the exit for **Gravelly Point/Roaches Run**, and you will enter a park adjacent to the Ronald Reagan Washington National Airport (DCA). Here you'll have **close encounters with jets (74)**, with giant jets taking off and landing in a flight path immediately east of you, overhead within a hundred yards. Anyone thrilled by a close-up photo of giant aircraft will enjoy this stop. Keep the aircraft in the center of your viewfinder as you snap the shutter. This "panning" strategy will keep the image of the aircraft steady as your camera and the aircraft move simultaneously, resulting in a crisp photo. Late afternoon/sunset is the ideal time to photograph here because the slanted light falls on the aircraft, which will fly past you only a short distance to the east.

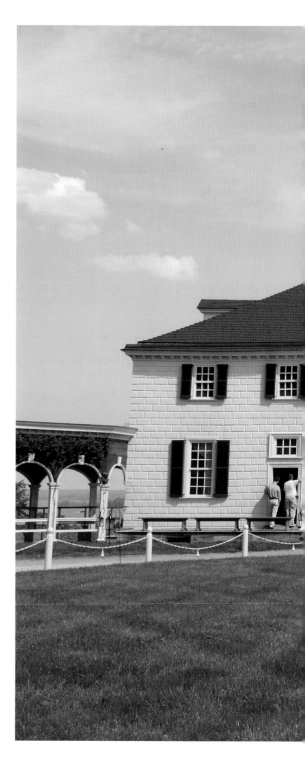

George Washington's home, Mount Vernon

Cherry blossoms and the Washington Monument

Favorites

Close-up of Abraham Lincoln statue

Most Satisfying Iconic Photos

Abraham Lincoln sculpture and his inscribed oratorical words, Lincoln Memorial

Golden afternoon light on the Capitol dome

Best Nature Photos

Spring color in April and May, hiking to the scenic overlook at Great Falls Park on the Potomac River

Fall color near the White House at 17th and E Streets NW, at Great Falls Park, and at Theodore Roosevelt Island

Most Inspiring Smithsonian Photos

The Wright Brothers' *Flyer* at the Air and Space Museum

The *Blackbird* spy plane at the Air and Space Udvar-Hazy Center

Best Festival Photos

Cherry blossoms at their peak in late March to early April on the Tidal Basin

July Fourth Fireworks from the Netherlands Carillon adjacent to the Iwo Jima Memorial

Best Quirky Only-in-Washington Photos

Jets taking off and landing at Gravelly Point Park/Roaches Run, adjacent to Washington National DCA Airport

Photograph jets close up at Gravelly Point Park near Washington National Airport

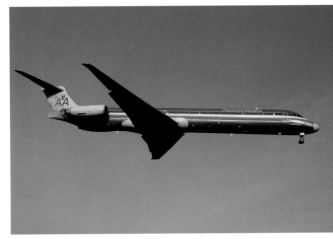

Chesapeake Bay blue crabs at the Maine Avenue Fish Market

Best Market Photos

Blue crabs at the Maine Avenue Fish Market

Ethnic art at the Eastern Market flea market

Best Neighborhood Hangouts for Photos

Kramerbooks in Dupont Circle

Rosemary's Thyme Bistro in Adams-Morgan

Best Beyond-the-City Photos

Mount Vernon, George Washington's home

Chesapeake Bay on an excursion boat

Most Poignant War Memorial Photos

Multigenerational families pushing World War II survivors in wheelchairs around the National World War II Memorial

Friends and relatives of Vietnam War dead doing rubbings of names at the Vietnam Veterans Memorial

Useful Web Sites

The primary tourism information Web site for Washington, D.C., is Washington.org (www.washington.org; 202-789-7000). A photographer will find much useful info here, from details on annual events, such as the Cherry Blossom Festival, to links to many of the major sites to be photographed. The Visitors Center at 1300 Pennsylvania Avenue NW has maps and brochures.

The Washington Monument and several memorials on the National Mall are administered by the **National Park Service**. Their informative Web site is www.nps.gov/nacc. Many further aspects of the national park presence around the city can also be accessed. Go to www.nps.gov, and search "Washington, D.C.,"

or search for any more specific idea you might want to research for a photographic outing.

The **Smithsonian Institution** is a vast resource of subjects interesting to the photographer. All 19 museums are described at www.si.edu, starting with Air and Space on the Mall, which is one of the most visited museums in the world. A consumer-friendly guide to the Smithsonian's main attractions, with maps, can be picked up in print and seen online at www.gosmithsonian.com, complete with turnable pages and maps showing the major Smithsonian attractions.

The Smithsonian's **National Air and Space Museum's Steven F. Udvar-Hazy Center,**

Taking the Metro is the best way to get around D.C.

Colorful house mural in the Adams-Morgan district

opened in 2003 near Dulles Airport, has many special aircraft to be photographed. For details, visit www.nasm.si.edu/museum/udvarhazy.

The most recent attraction in D.C. is also a glorious new photo platform. The **Newseum**, www.newseum.org, concerns itself with the media and its interaction with the public. The sixth-floor terrace offers a fresh late-afternoon photo angle of the Capitol and Pennsylvania Avenue, never possible before 2008.

Getting around the National Mall and downtown area will require some public transportation, cabs, or walking. One useful touring resource in the Mall area is **Tourmobile**, 888-868-7707, www.tourmobile.com. Their free all-day reboarding pass is worth considering. The Tourmobile also travels over to **Arlington National Cemetery** in Virginia.

Local tourism info for **Annapolis** and a trip to Chesapeake Bay is at www.visitannapolis.org.

The **Chesapeake & Ohio Canal**, known as the C&O, is a National Park Service jurisdiction. The C&O starts in Georgetown and offers plenty of outdoor and historic photo ideas. Full details are at www.nps.gov/choh. The **Great Falls Park** site on the C&O is a favored location for nature photos. Visit www.nps.gov/grfa.

Details for photos honoring the war dead at **Arlington National Cemetery** are at www.arlingtoncemetery.org.

When planning photos in **Alexandria's Old Town**, the helpful tourism Web site is www.visitalexandriava.com.

The **George Washington Memorial Parkway** has many photo-stop assets to consider, from the presidential home, Mount Vernon, at the south end to Great Falls on the C&O Canal at the north end. See it online at www.nps.gov/gwmp.